YE GODS!

JILL DUDLEY

TRAVELS IN GREECE

Published by
Orpington Publishers
Email: info@orpingtonpublishers.co.uk

Origination by
Creeds the Printers,
Broadoak, Dorset.
01308 423411

Cover design
and illustrations by
Clare E. Taylor

Printed by
J. H. Haynes & Co. Ltd.
Sparkford, Yeovil.
01963 440 635

ISBN 10: 0-9553834-0-4
ISBN 13: 978-0-9553834-0-3

CONTENTS

INTRODUCTION

Most travel books are written by adventurers who do all manner of daring things like crossing deserts, sailing oceans, travelling by donkey, camel, horse or bicycle. We, however, are anti-heroes. We travel cautiously which, perhaps, is why we have never returned on stretchers like a friend who, on his first night in Athens, strode confidently out from bed to bathroom and fell down a step and broke his leg. Although we came close to it we never, like him, found ourselves shunted around a hospital confronted by Greek doctors and nurses speaking their frantic, incomprehensible language.

I never thought when we first travelled there that Greece would get a hold of me. I went armed with the legends of the gods and immediately became bewitched by how much of the pagan past was still around today. It would have helped had Greece got a hold of Harry too; but he just tagged along to see he didn't lose me to some swarthy Greek.

To help me I learned Greek. "Why are you doing that?" friends would ask kindly. Why does anybody do anything? I had no good answer and would look helpless, gripped as I was by my own enthusiasm - 'enthusiasm' is a corruption of the old Greek meaning to be possessed by a god, a sort of giddyness, the word 'theos' meaning 'god' - 'en theos iasm'.

That we ever got away surprised me as I never expected any journey to come off but supposed always we'd be thwarted by some problem or sent obstacles to overcome as though by a divine hand testing me. Having got away, I was equally surprised when we got back again. And yet I'd say that I'm an optimist. Why else would I have planned these trips unless supposing they would come to pass?

This book, then, is about the visits we have made up mountains, to ancient temple sites and churches, to monasteries and caves and islands. It is about the people we have met; about their festivals and their beliefs and the ebb and flow of my own thoughts regarding faith, or lack of it.

CITY OF THE GODS

ATHENS

It was impossible to ignore the Greek woman with the rotund figure, sparse permed hair and lively eye. Until I smiled at her she had that air of aloof self-consciousness which solitary women in hotel dining-rooms tend to assume. We were at breakfast and I asked her if she would like to bring her coffee across. Harry pretended she didn't exist as he never speaks to foreigners if he can avoid it.

In typical Greek fashion she asked direct questions and learned we were from England, that Harry was a farmer and preferred his home comforts to tramping ancient sites; that I was a writer and so on. She told me she had come for the funeral of a beloved uncle; that she lived on the island of Chios, was a widow and had two grown offspring living in Australia.

She went on to say that if there was time between family obligations she would like to hire a taxi and take us to some far-flung seaside resort. "I will pay for the taxi," she went on hurriedly, seeing the alarm on Harry's face at the thought of the expense. "In Greece it is an honour to give hospitality. You understand?" When she learned I was interested in ancient sanctuaries, she suggested we go east to Sounion to the temple of Poseidon, god of the sea; or we could go west to Eleusis where the Eleusian Mysteries had taken place at the sanctuary of Demeter, goddess of corn, and from there on to Delphi.

Were we going to see the Parthenon, she enquired? She didn't think it would be open that morning. She called to the woman replenishing the coffee-pot at the serving table - would the Parthenon be open on Good Friday morning? Everyone would be in church, was that not so? I told her that I knew it was closed and planned to go to church myself - not because I was a believer but because I was looking for enlightenment and thought the Orthodox Church might help me.

Her eyes were restless, darting from my head to my left shoulder, to my neck, ear, hair, clothing - What were my views on the Elgin Marbles, she asked? Superb, I said, fearing Greek wrath at them being in England. I quickly deflected any anger by remarking that I thought as a supreme gesture of goodwill they should be returned to Greece. At least meanwhile they were safe, she said, her preparation for battle having been defused.

So where would I like to go if she had time on her hands, she asked again? Her eyes were still darting about me and I ignored the several sharp kicks Harry aimed at my shin under the table. Had we been to the Daphne Monastery a few miles away, or the Kaisariani Monastery in the Hymettos mountains nearby? I noted that her long taxi expedition was becoming considerably shorter. Why was I interested in the old gods at all, she asked?

When I told her that I found it strange that many of the Orthodox saints had names similar to the old gods she dismissed it outright, declaring that Christianity had nothing whatever to do with the pagan gods.

After half an hour of heated discussion regarding the Greek Orthodox Church, the Church of England and personal conviction or lack of it, she suddenly looked at her watch and sprang up. "Paw, paw, paw! It is late! We will talk more but now I must leave you. Tonight we will go together to see the procession of the Epitaphios. I will show you our customs here in Greece!"

We entered a small Byzantine church for the Good Friday morning service. I wanted to see how those who had once been pagan in Athens celebrated Easter. The interior of Orthodox churches, and the old Byzantine ones in particular, are exquisite with their mosaics, icons, frescoes and richly carved and gilded iconostasis (the icon-covered sanctuary screen).

I was struck by the numbers in the church on this Good Friday morning. I tried to think good thoughts and not to ask absurd questions about the Almighty and why he had sent his Son into the world in order to save sinners. Men had never stopped sinning and, if anything, were sinning more than ever. Why should they be saved anyway?

Before the sanctuary was a decorated Epitaphios (a representation of Christ's tomb). It was on a stand enshrouded in white satin and consisted of diagonal arches smothered in small white flower-heads; the whole was topped with a flower bedecked crown and small cross. Prominently placed was a painted wooden replica of the crucified Christ attached to a plain dark wooden cross.

A woman suddenly prostrated herself at the foot of

the cross. Nobody paid her the slightest attention and I supposed she must have broken some commandment. I couldn't imagine ever prostrating myself in that way however guilty I felt. In fact the more guilty I was the less would I want to draw attention to it in that manner. This was my second Easter that year. Easter in England had been two weeks earlier because the West uses the Gregorian calendar whilst the Orthodox Church uses the old Julian one for celebrating Easter.

At the beginning of Holy Week in England I had telephoned the vicar to explain that I wanted to attend all the services that year, not because of any sudden religious conviction but because I was agnostic and wanted to try to understand the Christian message. The vicar had been very kind, possibly very pleased that anybody was coming at all. At the first service of the Stations of the Cross (newly introduced to the parish by him) I had been the only one there. It had been awkward just the two of us, but he had bravely taken me through the story of Christ's Passion picture by picture with the relevant readings and prayers. At the end I had thanked him and said: "Well, I believe in the holy breath of life," or some such footling remark, to which he had kindly replied, "Well, that's a good start anyway."

Here in Athens a church elder was bringing in a stepladder and placing it beside the cross. He climbed up and began to remove the screws holding Christ to it whilst the priest and deacon stood below with a white cloth laid across their outstretched arms ready to receive the body. There was a lot of sniffing and blowing of noses and I thought, 'Oh, hell, there's a virus flying around Athens and I'll catch it.' But then the man in front trumpeted into a handkerchief and wiped his eyes and I realized they were weeping. Nobody had wept in England. But then very few had gone to church except on Easter Sunday, the day of the Resurrection.

The service seemed to be going on forever and I left before the end. I found Harry sitting on a wall reading a book.

"Oh, there you are," Harry said. "Have you done your church-going?"

"Yes, for the time being," I answered.

"Plenty more time for this, I expect," he said, closing his book. "On to the next site then." And he got up, resigned that here in this second Holy Week there would still be more churches (or sanctuaries) to be visited.

That night the pavements of Ermou Street were cordoned off and all traffic diverted. Along a side street units from the armed forces waited for the main procession of the Epitaphios which would come from the cathedral. Outside the cathedral Greek flags fluttered and the street lamps were shrouded in black crepe.

It was getting dark and there were crowds lining the route. Children were selling yellow candles - yellow for mourning, we were told by Kuria (Mrs.) Alezaki (the woman who had befriended us that morning at our hotel).

A man standing beside us in the waiting crowds began to speak about the route the procession would take. He spoke good English and I asked him if he knew England. He said he should by now as he had worked in London twenty years, but always returned to Greece for Easter. Wasn't Christmas as important, I asked? Christmas didn't compare, he said; everyone was born but few were crucified and Christ's crucifixion and Resurrection were unique. I was impressed by his faith.

"If you can accept the death and resurrection of Dionysos, then it is not so difficult to believe in the death and Resurrection of the Lord," said Kuria Alezaki, and she stroked my shoulder in a kindly compassionate way. "And it is the same with the story of Demeter (goddess of corn) and her daughter," she said.

I'd mentioned these resurrections to her when we'd been discussing the subject of gods and resurrections at the hotel, but she'd dismissed it outright as being nothing more than symbolic of the natural life-cycle of plants.

An order was shouted and the army stood to attention. A bell began to toll. "There! they are coming now, see?" said Kuria Alezaki and she went up on her toes to get a better view.

The army presented arms to the cross as it was brought from the cathedral. It was followed by a very large Epitaphios which was shaped something like a coronation coach and smothered in small white flower-heads.

A band struck up a funeral march whilst the cathedral bell tolled in mourning. It was like a great Puccini opera unfolding before us. Kuria Alezaki blew her nose and wiped her eyes. "Every year I feel it here in my heart! Those of my family who are dead, you understand." Recovering her composure Kuria Alezaki used my shoulder to steady herself as she stood tiptoe. Four bearded priests in damask robes, with their tall black headgear and black veils at the back, carried between them a replica coffin covered by a gold and purple encrusted pall with rose petals scattered over it. They were followed by bishops in magnificent attire with their bejewelled gold and silver dome-shaped mitres. Behind came several rows of dark-suited government officials bearing candles.

We followed the procession for a while and I saw that Harry with his candle was also caught up in this Greek celebration. The flame cast a light on his half smiling must-do-as-the-Greeks-do expression. Kuria Alezaki had a fixed look of piety on her face. We ended up in a church where Kuria Alezaki beckoned to me to follow her lead, putting the thumb to the first two fingers and making the sign of the cross over the breast the Orthodox way (the Roman Catholics do it differently, and Harry didn't do it at all). She kissed several icons and lit a candle of supplication which I also did. Under her guidance I felt quite holy.

On our way back to the hotel a near catastrophe occurred serving as a reminder of our mortality. We were walking along a narrow pavement in a badly lit street when I heard a scratchy, slithering sound behind me and a thump. When I turned I found Harry on his back.

God! he'd had a heart-attack? "Are you all right?" - silly question when he clearly wasn't. Was he breathing? Was he alive even?

He was alive because he said: "Think so - slipped up on something."

"Are you in pain?" He was sitting on the pavement flexing his leg. It turned out he had stepped on a metal beer-bottle cap which had slithered away taking him with it.

Kuria Alezaki and I helped him up and I gave silent thanks to the god or saint or guardian angel who had kept Harry from doing worse damage to himself. We were not far from the hotel and with our assistance he was able to flinch and hop his way back to it.

"It is because he does not light the candle or kiss

the icon," said Kuria Alezaki privately to me afterwards. "It is better that you do these things or perhaps next time he breaks the leg."

The following day Harry felt he could limp along with me to the Acropolis. He hopped along the old alleyways of Plaka. It was pleasantly uncrowded, many people having left the city for the islands and villages. The alleyways were festooned with bright red Easter eggs strung across between houses, giving everything a festive air.

The weather was warm and the sky unusually blue and free of the smog which usually hangs above Athens. A few shredded white clouds scudded across the sky.

We approached the Parthenon and I hoped that I wouldn't find her a bit of a wreck as I had on my first visit some years before. But on this occasion I was in a spring-like, more receptive mood. I sat on a marble block and found her rather wonderful, in fact totally majestic. Had I lived in pagan times I would, no doubt, have come and done honour to the goddess Athena in return for her divine protection.

"There! You've seen the Parthenon," said Harry, ready to move on.

"Wait! We've only just got here," I objected. "Have you got the binoculars?"

He unslung them from his neck and handed them over before seating himself patiently on another marble block.

To me the fascination with the Parthenon was its conversion from being the temple of Athena, goddess of wisdom, to becoming the city's cathedral dedicated to Agia Sophia (Holy Wisdom). Later it became known as the Panagia Atheniotissa, the All Holy Lady of Athens. By this subtle use of language the pagan mind had been drawn into Christianity.

When I'd first told Harry of these learned discoveries he'd merely shrugged and said, 'Well, what did you expect?' The fact was I hadn't expected anything as I hadn't thought at all. I had always supposed that Christianity had stamped itself once and for all as soon as the apostles had gone about preaching 'in tongues' under the influence of the Holy Spirit. That Christianity had taken hundreds of years to establish itself had never been part of my education.

I scanned the inner wall of the Parthenon where I understood the faintest traces of a fresco of the Virgin Mary could be detected from its Christian days. But I could see nothing from my position beyond the cordon which kept visitors at a distance.

"What are you looking for?" Harry enquired.

"A fresco of the Virgin Mary," I replied.

"That's ridiculous."

"Not really." And I explained the reason why I kept twiddling the knobs to get a clearer focus. In the end I gave up on the Virgin Mary who didn't want to be found.

I studied the metopes (sculptured panels between triglyphs in the frieze below the pediment). I had read that the zeal of Christians had caused many of the figures to be defaced. One, however, had been left untouched because it was thought to resemble the Christian notion of the Virgin Mary being visited by the angel Gabriel at the Annunciation. Well - maybe.

I turned my attention to the Erechtheum, the small temple on the north side of the Acropolis with its caryatid maidens supporting the roof with their eyes towards the Parthenon. I tried to find traces in this of the old conversion to a church which had taken place also in the sixth century, making two churches on the Acropolis. But I could see nothing.

It was there that the goddess Athena had competed with Poseidon for the patronage of the city. It is said that Athena won by presenting the people with the olive tree, something far superior to Poseidon's somewhat hopeless gift who, by striking the rock with his trident, had brought salt water gushing from the ground. It was the precious oil from Athena's olive that became the prize awarded to the winners of the Panathenaic Games.

Athena's Panathenaia Festival had been an annual event held mid-summer to commemorate her birth - a birth most strange as she had sprung fully armed from the head of Zeus, supreme god of the ancient world. The Elgin marbles portray the procession at the Panathenaia and depict magnificent sculptured figures of young girls, priests, youths on horseback, marshals, heifers for sacrifice and the folded newly woven garment to be presented to the cult statue of the goddess on this her mid-summer festival. Today the major mid-summer festival of the Orthodox Church (surprise, surprise!) is in honour of the Virgin Mary. It was introduced in the sixth century by the Emperor Mauricius (Maurice).

As there was still time that morning to look in at the cathedral, I steered Harry in that direction. As we approached, however, he smelt a rat and declared that enough was enough for one morning and he was going back to the hotel. I watched Harry hopping off into the distance along Ermou Street, then climbed the steps to the cathedral.

The nineteenth century cathedral wasn't the most attractive of buildings. The ground was strewn with laurel leaves, originally of significance in the worship of Apollo and now symbolic of Christ's victory over death. Above the door to the sanctuary was a single eye surrounded by the rays of the sun - the watching eye, the rising sun, the light of the world.

Around the great candle-sticks and the hanging candelabra were tied black and mauve ribbons of mourning. A service was coming to an end and a priest was administering the sacraments from a chalice to the last of the communicants. Many people were departing with cubes of bread (the bread of Christian fellowship).

Unlike the western Church which has individual wafers, the Orthodox Church has a loaf of bread and whatever isn't used for the sacraments is cut up and distributed to all comers as a mark of Christian fellowship. I always ate the bread supposing it would trigger good Christian thoughts; Harry, though, regarded it as germ-ridden and tended to throw it away to birds or starving cats.

If Harry took Christianity on trust but lacked reverence, I had the latter but a severe lack of comprehension. Maybe it stemmed from my first communion when I'd taken the bread and wine and had expected a roll of drums or a sudden visionary light but had received neither.

The communicants were thinning out and only a few people were left. I hovered uncertainly near the chancel steps wondering whether I was allowed to take the sacraments in this Orthodox cathedral - whether it might do me good and produce the understanding I was searching after.

Soon I stood alone and the eyes of the priest above the black bushy beard and below the black eyebrows rested on me. I gave him an enquiring look and pointed to myself but, slowly and with dignity, the priest turned away and I was left a solitary and miserable - well, really quite a happy - sinner, wondering about salvation.

It was evident that Kuria Alezaki was worried about my soul. "You ask too many questions," she scolded, taking my arm as we made our way to the small Byzantine Church of Agia Aikaterini below the Acropolis for the Resurrection service. I had told her that I wanted to be in a church near to the Parthenon because I wanted to experience Christianity close to the temple of Athena. Harry had decided he didn't want to go to church at all.

"How can you think of the goddess Athena on this night?" Kuria Alezaki complained. "When you love do you ask if your love is the love of Helen of Troy? Faith is like love. We know what love is when we give ourselves to it. But it becomes difficult if you think only of an old love who is dead. Because you are my friend I can say this to you." She was walking unsteadily in high-heeled shoes beside me. Her shoes had adornments at the back which looked like bicycle reflectors, something which was considered very chic in Greece at the time.

We arrived at the small Byzantine Church of Agia Aikaterini. There were already many people there. St. Paul had been right when he had visited Athens and had said that he could see they were a very religious people. At the time he had been preaching to them about Jesus and the Resurrection but they had been unable to understand what he was talking about. Perhaps they still didn't understand but just went along with it.

Kuria Alezaki said: "Come now. If you do as I do this will be good for you." She drew me forward and began to set an example of Orthodox piety, lighting a candle, making numerous signs of the cross and kissing various icons.

"Please - excuse us, my friend from England wishes to see the Resurrection -" And she gradually drew me forward through the crush till we were near the iconostasis.

The glistening mosaics reflected the light from the many candles. The glinting brass chandeliers and ancient icons, the gleaming white marble pulpit and the carved and gilded bishop's throne, all exuded a feeling of sanctity in this small Byzantine church.

Here the central doors to the iconostasis was a sliding door and it was now tested on its runners. On it Christ was depicted holding a chalice. He slid from view as the door was drawn aside; a moment later he slid back into view, closing off the sanctuary. The sliding door was rather like my faith, there one moment, gone the next.

Julian the Apostate, Roman Emperor from 361 A.D., had been brought up a Christian but had given up on it and had returned to the old gods. He had been an intellectual and had pitted his wits against the Christian claims as he found them impossible to believe. He had no time to turn the tide back to paganism, however, as he was killed by an arrow at the age of thirty-one which some might say was a clear sign of divine retribution.

Just before midnight the antiphonal chanting between priest and psaltoi built up to a climax. The lights in the church were switched off leaving all in darkness except for the glimmer of four icon lamps hanging before the iconostasis. There was an air of increasing expectancy. Kuria Alezaki handed me a white candle and with a gesture indicated to me to prepare to follow her lead.

Midnight!

The central door of the iconostasis slid back and, against the black interior of the sanctuary, the bearded priest in rich vestments stood before the altar holding a single lighted candle. He advanced and pronounced the words: "Christos anestei!" (Christ is risen!).

At the same moment the church bells pealed deafeningly in sharp bursts and fire-crackers were let off outside. I was thrust forward by Kuria Alezaki to light my candle from the priest's new 'Light of the world'. There was a certain honour in receiving it direct from the priest and then lighting the candles of other people behind.

When we emerged, having pushed our way through the crush, I was astonished to find there were as many people in the courtyard and in the surrounding streets as in the church. All had been listening to the service relayed to them from loud-speakers.

Guarding our candles against the strong breeze which blew the flames sideways, we began to return to our hotel. The narrow street along which we walked was congested with people and cars, all of which had their windows shut to protect the flames of those inside holding candles. It is a sign of good fortune if you can get back with it still alight. I tried not to be hopelessly superstitious when my candle blew out three times.

We turned a corner and suddenly I saw the Parthenon floodlit and resplendent in its gold white light against the night sky. It seemed that the old protectress of the city was not forgotten and she still had her place in the hierarchy of things. All was a celebration that night with the old and the new co-existing happily side by side.

"Now we crack eggs together as is the custom in Greece!" said Kuria Alezaki glancing at my hair, my ear, my nose and eyebrow. We were sitting at breakfast and she handed me a red egg. Harry rather spoiled things by saying he didn't want an egg but only cereal.

"You must hold yours up like I do," she said, ignoring Harry. "Now I say 'Christos anestei!'" She cracked her egg against mine, "and you reply 'Aleithos anestei!'"

The words were rattled off so fast I was unable to pick up on them and so hesitated. "Say it! say it as I have taught you! 'Aleithos anestei!'" ordered Kuria Alezaki.

A little girl at a nearby table squirmed with delight and lifted up a red egg hoping to crack hers too. "You see? You are keeping everybody waiting!" scolded Kuria Alezaki. "Come! come!" and she beckoned the child to join us and ordered me to crack it with the young girl.

"Christos anestei!" whispered the child.

"Aleithos anestei!" prompted Kuria Alezaki, her eyes looking at mine for once before darting to my hair.

"Aleithos anestei!" I repeated obediently.

"Bravo! You say it with the true Greek accent too!"

Everybody smiled and nodded and I could see that I had pleased the child with my reply.

"What the hell was all that about?" asked Harry afterwards when we were back in our room.

"Kuria Alezaki was saying 'Christ is risen!'"

"And what was it you had to say?"

"He is risen indeed!"

"Well, that's a first coming from you!" said Harry. "You'll be singing in the choir next! Heaven forbid!" Then, like a conjurer pulling rabbits out of a hat, he took two hard-boiled eggs from one trouser pocket and from the other several rolls, butter and cheese wrapped in paper table-napkins which he had secreted from the serving table. "Our lunch," he said.

The idea was to take a taxi into the Hymettos mountains. Harry thought he could limp amongst the wild flowers and have a picnic. Much to his relief Kuria Alezaki was being received into the bosom of her family and would not be free to take us around Attica.

In the Hymettos I hoped to see the Kaisariani Monastery, an eleventh century building built on the site of a fifth century Christian basilica which itself had been built on the site of shrines erected to the gods - in particular to Aphrodite. There Aphrodite had had a sacred spring, source of the Ilissos river, which had once supplied Athens with her drinking water.

I was already planning another trip in pursuit of gods and goddesses and an understanding of Christianity. Next time we would go north to Mt. Olympus and from there on to see the remnants of Dionysiac worship at Langadhás.

MOUNTAIN OF THE GODS

CHAPTER

2

MT. OLYMPUS

It was mid-May when we flew to Greece again. We travelled by train to Larissa from Athens. As we approached Lamia, a woman in our carriage started up a conversation and in rapid Greek told me either that her husband was swimming in the sea or that he was responsible for washing olives. She kept pointing to the concrete troughs of water on the outskirts of the town and repeating the words 'banio' (bathe or bath) and 'thalassa' (sea) until I became hopelessly confused.

The train stopped and I amused myself by unravelling the Greek lettering on the station wall. 'Larissa', I read. I hadn't bargained on the train arriving one hour early. From there we had to catch a bus for Litochoro at the foot of Mt. Olympus. Harry was asleep. He never knows where we are going as he leaves the planning of these trips to me.

I woke Harry urgently and we quickly gathered our belongings and leaped down on the track where a number of workmen were leaning on picks and shovels watching us. At that time Greece's railway network was really very simple; there were tracks going up and tracks coming down. Rail costs were kept to a minimum by dispensing with such unnecessary things as platforms, railway crossings and subways. The Greeks travelled cheaply and at their own risk. They put their faith in the Almighty or believed their fate lay in the lap of the gods - it is interesting that people still talk either way.

When we finally arrived we found Litochoro to be a pleasant little garrison town with a church in its plateia and shops lining its steep, narrow streets. The town lies on the lower slopes of Mt. Olympus like a child on the lap of a great matriarchal figure. It is perched close to where the Epineas river breaks cover from the mountain and meanders off along the lower flat terrain to the sea.

That night we sat outside a taverna in the cold. Somehow we felt this was appropriate to Greece whose brochures advertised sunshine and warmth. The young men of the town sensibly stayed inside, their attentions riveted to a television set up on a wall where an action-packed Western was being shown. By now my eye, which had been watering profusely from the grit and dust of Athens, had recovered but if I was constantly blowing my nose it was because I'd caught a cold. I was torn between telling Harry in order to get sympathy or keeping silent, which isn't always easy with a cold. I didn't want him sabotaging my plan to climb Olympus.

I managed to control a sneeze and discreetly blew my nose. "You'll be glad to hear my eye's cured," I said to Harry who showed little interest in something that was by now all right. Instead, he said: "I'd better put another plaster on my finger - don't want that to get infected." He had earlier cut it on his Swiss army knife whilst slicing a piece of cheese.

By morning my cold was worse, the day was fine but rain was forecast. Now that we'd arrived, however, it was unthinkable that we should abandon climbing the mountain. We were only there for that one purpose and, as we had deadlines to be met, it had to be then or not at all.

"Please to ask the driver if the rain it comes," said a German girl from the Youth Hostel. We were in a taxi bumping along the pot-holed road from Litochoro to the trail-head at Prionia where climbers begin the trek up the mountain. I asked in Greek and the driver raised his hands to heaven as he manoeuvred slowly between a fresh rock-fall on one side and a precipice filled with conifers on the other. We didn't know the others in the taxi but had met them at the taxi-stand in Litochoro and we had agreed to do the fifteen kilometres together.

A student, whom we were soon to nickname 'the Scholar', assured us that even if it rained the peaks of Olympus would be up above the clouds 'to the brilliance that is there outspread' - a quote from The Iliad, she said. She had a plain face and sallow complexion enhanced by thin-rimmed spectacles.

By the time we reached the trail-head the pinnacles of ragged rock, some snow-capped and streaked with crevices of snow, were masked by cloud and glimpsed only occasionally as we began to follow the trail up. The track took us through the lower slopes of pine and beech trees, the latter fresh with their new spring foliage. Here and there were carpets of flowers: violets, grape-hyacinth, forget-me-not, iris and lily of the valley.

The German girl said that she had had much experience of walking in the mountains at high altitudes and we should take it slowly. "To walk and then the rest, this is something I know," she said. "The drink, this is important and when you sit and you are hot the jersey you must wear."

Her German boy-friend stood smiling protectively beside her or plodded up a few feet behind. We tramped steadily upwards and soon the gorge lay way below, a chasm of trees. After half an hour we were already tired and hot and perched ourselves on a rock and obediently put on jerseys. We could see the heads of the two Germans slowly ascending a hundred yards or so below.

"You've read Hesiod's Theogony, of course, about the battle of the gods?" asked the Scholar. And without waiting for an answer she waved an arm at the mountain and began declaiming like a great Shakespearean actress something about the earth crashing loudly, the broad sky quaking and Olympus being shaken to its foundations by the onrush of immortal gods. Her words echoed around the mountain. We admired her oratory and learned she was destined to read classics up at Oxford.

A short rest and we continued with our upward climb. I had been told that any fool could climb the mountain. But a narrow track past a steep incline made me want to cling forever to the nearest boulder for fear of swinging like a pendulum over the edge. Down the slope a number of uprooted conifers lay like spillikins amongst fallen rocks revealing how a storm or avalanche in winter could change the face of the mountain (or the climber) in an instant. But having got so far I believed in my destiny. It was surely ordained that I should climb the mountain of the

gods. Why else had   we got so far?   I could imagine
the Olympian deities lurking everywhere watching our
progress.

   We reached a forest of firs and, as we looked down
through the trees stretching away into the depths with
their tall, slender trunks throwing out their branches to
each other; and as the Scholar pointed out that we were
now at last above a canopy of clouds 'to the brilliance
that is there outspread', her statement quite collapsed as
the cloud below suddenly billowed up through the trees
and swirled ghost-like amongst the thickly pine-needled
branches until we too were engulfed.

   By now my cold had become a croak. "You've got
a cold?" Harry suddenly noticed. But at that instant
he had a nose-bleed and was more concerned with his
predicament than mine. "Rarefied atmosphere," Harry
mumbled through a tissue. As usual he was realistic and
had a scientific explanation for such problems. I, on the
other hand, read into everything signs and omens, in this
instance a warning we should turn back. But to give up
now and return down seemed worse than carrying on.

   Staunching our various ailments we struggled on up
the narrow track against a mounting wind and rain. After
what seemed like many hours into our climb, we at last
saw high above us, the railings around the rocky ledge on
which the Spilios Agapitos refuge-hut was perched.

   We slogged on upwards, crossing a wide ravine of
hard-packed snow, spurred on by the knowledge that we
had glimpsed our goal and we were nearly there. Hail now
stung our faces and the wind was icy. Then suddenly we
had arrived. The refuge-hut was a bungalow-type building
managed with supreme efficiency by a husband and wife
team.

Inside the refectory a log fire blazed and damp clothes steamed from the mantelpiece where they'd been hung to dry. Our supper was hot potato stew which we devoured, together with a bottle of red wine.

Various groups sat at refectory tables and, as they tucked into their plates of food and drank beer or wine, they talked of their adventures. We were a cosmopolitan bunch of about twenty and all had been drawn to the mountain inspired by the legends of antiquity. They spoke of their feelings of triumph and the awesome wonder of being on top of the mountain. Some had that afternoon been where the gods had once held court. From there they had seen the huge scallop-shaped rock known as the Throne of Zeus - Zeus, supreme god of the ancient world; Zeus the 'cloud gatherer' and thrower of thunderbolts, the bringer of rain. It seemed he was still powerful as rain splattered on the window-panes and streamed from the gutters.

We were given a small room to ourselves. There were two beds tucked under a sloping ceiling with a tiny window opposite. I took pills and lozenges and rolled myself in blankets. My head felt as if a pagan god was sitting on my nose and I couldn't sleep. I tossed about with constant visions of dizzy heights and precipices. At around midnight I was aware that the rain had stopped. Would we be going higher then? The thought of having done it was much better than the thought of doing it.

I fell asleep at last but woke up with a start because I was falling into a ravine. I saw it was now five o'clock. As I lay awake trying not to worry about the higher slopes, I realized suddenly that my cold had gone. It was as though some unseen hand had in the night swept it from me. So it was true what they said about the Greeks who'd held out against the Turks in their War of Independence; then they'd made a point of coming to the mountain in the belief that the icy Mt. Olympus air and springs would heal their wounds and imbue them with renewed vigour and a fresh fighting spirit.

A voice came out of the darkness. "Are you awake?"

"Yes."

Harry's voice was glum: "Haven't slept at all. My back's kaput." So it wasn't true.

I said: "Poor you."

"Don't know if I can get out of bed even," came the mournful voice.

The generator started and the lights came on. I unrolled myself from my blankets thinking with some relief that that put paid to going higher to the Mytikas Peak. I helped heave Harry to a sitting position, then watched as he lowered his feet to the ground. I gave him pain killers, a massage and what encouragement I could, before hurrying to the wash-house which was down a flight of steps and accessible only from the terrace outside. I wanted to get there before the general stampede from those sleeping in the dormitory.

I leaned on the railings and watched the sunrise. The ravines and gorges below were blanketed in a white magnesium mist whilst the craggy peaks behind were starkly silhouetted with the first rays of sunlight on them.

The Scholar appeared beside me. She was waxy faced and dishevelled and had a towel thrown over her shoulder. Without her spectacles her eyes blinked as though the early morning light was too strong for them. We leaned on the railings together as the sun rose.

The German girl joined us. "Guten morgan. It rains today again, Helmut he tells me. He already higher goes.

Do you higher go this day?"

I told them about Harry's predicament and they commiserated and repeated the comforting words of rain or even snow on the higher slopes.

I returned to our room and found Harry sitting on the edge of his bed attempting to put on a sock, swinging it out like a butterfly-net to trap his toes.

"I feel thwarted," I said.

"That makes two of us," he remarked, throwing the sock out and this time hooking it to his foot. I helped him on with his sock. "I really, really want to get up to the Throne of Zeus."

"We'll be lucky if we get lower, that's all I know."

Realizing there was no question of doing it but feeling frustrated by obstacles, I added: "And the Chapel of the Profitis Hlias."

"Profitis what?"

"Hlias - Elijah."

"Whatever for?"

"Because - well, he was at Christ's Transfiguration," I said somewhat pointlessly.

The chapel was on a high peak where there'd formerly been a shrine to Zeus. I was interested that Hlias was similar to the Greek word 'helios' (sun) and there seemed to be a decided connection between mountain peaks, the sun, the prophet and Zeus. In ancient times Zeus had had shrines on high mountain peaks which were replaced by chapels to the Profitis Hlias - something any traveller to Greece will testify. Zeus was controller of the weather and it seemed to me significant that in Greece, where rain was sometimes scarce, his authority had been superseded by the prophet who had once brought a three year drought to an end by his faith in God. There was a sort of visual similarity also between Elijah who had been drawn up to heaven in a chariot of fire and the chariot portrayed in the Elgin Marbles drawing Helios (the sun) up into the heavens.

After dressing and getting to the wash-house Harry found he wasn't a complete cripple and his back began to ease. At least we'd be able to get down, he said. We had breakfast at a refectory table beside the blazing log fire and relaxed over cups of coffee.

Others at our table spoke glibly of the various routes they'd done around the mountain during the summer months. They told me of a north-east trail which led to the Plateau of the Muses where there was another small refuge-hut, the Christos Kakalos.

I told them how one day I'd like to do the trail until they spoke about a narrow ridge that had to be crossed. I could do it on a mule, I suggested?

"A mule?" It was Harry speaking. "You wouldn't be any good on a mule!"

A wiry Greek voiced what I myself would otherwise have said: "Why not?"

"She's never ridden a mule in her life," he remarked, breaking his rule of never speaking to foreigners.

My wiry Greek assessed the situation, then admitted that there might be a problem. It was at this narrow ledge beside a precipice that mules had to be dismounted and led on a tight rein, and if I didn't like heights and didn't ride mules... He regarded me with sorrowful amusement, then gave an upward jerk of the head and went 'tst' which is the Greek way of saying 'no'. Another dream was vanishing.

They told me about another refuge-hut called Apostolidhi a little higher than the Christos Kakalos, which was on a saddle joining the Profetis Hlias peak to the Throne of Zeus. On a fine night the sky was a canopy of stars, as though thousands of crystal chandeliers hung in the darkness. They were playing with me; they could see my appetite was whetted.

Yes, there had been fatalities on the mountain, the die-hard walkers said in answer to my question. One of the worst passages for novice climbers was near the top along a ridge where there was a drop of some five hundred metres. Down there amongst craggy rocks, clouds formed and boiled up with unexpected suddenness. It was called Kazania (Cauldrons) and at this point many who were unused to mountaineering were overcome by vertigo.

To reach the summit on a fine summer's day was, indeed, to see the 'brilliance that is there outspread'. The panoramic views from there extended to a radius of two hundred kilometres, no exaggeration, they said.

The German walked into the room and his girl-friend gave a whoop of joy. Questions and answers flew back and forth in German before she turned to me and said: "Helmut, he goes not up because it is ice - small ice rain - how you say?"

"Hail?" I said.

"Yes, yes, the hail and snow. It is not goot. We walk now down. You come?"

Feeling cheated of my inability to fulfil mountaineering feats, but glad the weather forecast was releasing me from any sense of guilt, I bought a postcard of the refuge-hut, and the manager and his wife stamped it on the back and signed it as proof of our having spent the night amongst the gods.

In the company of the Scholar and the German couple we descended Mt. Olympus. Now we were on the downward path Harry's back seemed miraculously cured and he strode along without a care in the world. As we set off I gave a silent prayer to the Almighty, promising to believe in him forever if he would get us safely across the ravine of hard-packed snow; I was convinced by now it must be undermined by all the rain in the night, that we would start an avalanche as soon as we set foot on it, and would be swept away with it into the abyss and oblivion.

We came to the dreaded snow. The German girl said: "Ach, there is no problem!" She had just told me about the casualties the manager of the refuge-hut had had to cope with: broken arms, legs and hypothermia, as well as fatalities. "Believe me, I have much experience walking in the mountains. You dig the heels in so, and do not look down. You follow me now!"

I kept my eyes on her footprints, dug my heels into the snow and began the trek across. I was half way over when I heard Harry behind me say, "My God! just look at that!"

I gave a downward glance. It was like looking from the top of a roller-coaster poised ready to descend to the unseen. The snow was splattered with broken branches, the conifers on either side shattered by fallen boulders. I quickly averted my eyes and focused on the German girl plodding ahead 'taking it slowly' with her 'much experience of walking in the mountains'.

Once we were across I felt a great burden lift off me, and my promise to the Almighty to believe in him for ever quickly evaporated in the Mt. Olympus air; instead, I imagined once again the immortal gods inhabiting their awesome mountain. In my mind's eye I could see almighty Zeus on his rocky throne in consultation with his fellow gods, discussing with them how best to stop the aspirations of the small band of impudent human visitors come to see his mountain, intent on climbing to his throne. Rain, of course! Hail and snow!

"Got a good quote for all this?" I asked the Scholar jokingly, when later we stood at a vantage point staring over cloud covered forest ranges of mountain peaks. The sun was shining on it and the mists were beginning to break up, causing the tops of the conifers to appear mysteriously. There was a great feeling of awe and majesty. After gazing for a while she told me that when the Trojan War was at its height and the Greeks were in danger of losing the battle, the goddess Hera had come in a chariot to petition Zeus (her husband) on Olympus. She again stretched out an arm to the sky and quoted from The Iliad something about Hera quickly touching the horses with a whip and the gates of heaven groaning open, the gates kept by the Seasons, who have charge over the heavens and Olympus, and who push the heavy cloud apart or close them.

She stopped as a stocky man in a small Tyrolean hat and leather shorts came climbing up the track. He was sweating profusely. "It is far?" he enquired, puffing heavily and leaning on a thick stick.

"Another two hours, perhaps three," I said, pleased to be going the other way. He gave a guttural grunt and heaved himself on upwards.

"The legs it is bad to walk too quick the mountain to come down," warned the German girl as she caught up with us. "Believe me what I say to you. I walk much on the mountains and it is more goot to walk down slow like so."

But we no longer cared how we walked now we were on the downward path. On our way the Scholar spoke of the wonderful manner in which the blind bard, Homer, had woven his heroes with the gods of Olympus and how in the Trojan War each had favoured one side or another. I said that they seemed to me to have been guardian angels. I mentioned the fact that I was discovering that many Greek Orthodox saints had names similar to the old gods of Olympus and that far from being ousted many had reappeared as Christian saints.

"Well, I wouldn't know about that!" said the Scholar dismissively.

But I wasn't to be so easily put off and told her how it had been Eusebius in his History of the Church, written in the early fourth century, who first drew my attention to the many early martyrs and saints with names similar to the Olympian deities. There had even been a martyr by the name of Zeus.

We'd reached the Prionia refuge and had already consumed bowls of hot bean soup when the German girl and her boy-friend arrived down. "You walk too quick the mountain to come down," she admonished. "Tomorrow you have the pain here in the leg, see?" She pointed to her thighs. What did it matter what happened tomorrow? We'd been in the world of gods but were at last safely back in the land of mortals where we belonged. Tomorrow was another day.

The German girl was right. The next morning the sinews and ligaments of our thighs were stretched taut like violin strings, ready to snap at the slightest awkward movement. We now hobbled into breakfast and eased ourselves painfully into sitting positions. A party of Germans was occupying two tables centrally placed nearby, bandying witticisms at each other. In contrast, beyond them sat an elderly couple in silence. The man looked like a professor with flat, sparse grey hair, drooping eyelids and a morose mouth. Across from him with her back to us was his wife, in a blue and white cotton blouse and jeans. She had short white hair brushed up and away from her face, and was eating toast and marmalade in a precise, neat manner. Clearly she was quite used to her silent and glum spouse opposite.

We began to make plans for the day and I told Harry how I would like to see an early monastery, the Monastery of Dionysios, on the lower slopes of the mountain. This was to be a pagan-god-come-Christian-saint investigation. I was interested because I'd read that Dionysos (pagan god of wine) had been worshipped in the locality.

Eventually, the Germans rose and began to file out, and I returned a polite 'Good morning' to their 'guten morgans'. The elderly couple rose too, and I thought I heard the word 'yes', but was not too sure. They looked neither to left nor right as they went out. The landlady entered to clear the tables and I asked her whether the two who had just gone were English. An instant later she had brought a passport, and I inquisitively turned the pages and read: Professor - , British subject.

Jumping immediately to the conclusion that he must know everything about archaeology or Byzantine studies, and had been sent by the gods for my benefit, I seized the first opportunity to speak to him.

I saw them emerging from their bedroom. He came first and his wife shut the door after him - a lifetime of silent attendance on this academic. They reminded me of a couple of oysters enclosed in their own small world.

"Good morning," I said. There was no immediate response, and I went closer. "I do hope you don't mind my asking, but you are English I believe? I heard you speaking in the dining-room," I lied.

The professor regarded me from under his drooping lids, as though I were some curious species to be viewed through binoculars from a great distance.

"I apologize for intruding on you like this, but I'm wondering whether by any chance you know anything about the Monastery of Dionysios - the old one on Mt. Olympus?" I asked.

His wife continued to fumble with the key in the lock. Without looking at me the Oyster remarked curtly: "Fifteenth century, I am told." He turned back to his wife with his hand out, and said: "Give me the key before you lose it." He took the key and thrust it into his jacket pocket.

The Oyster's wife was animated by this sudden intrusion into her quiet world. She was as fresh and alive as her husband was morose.

"Did I hear you say the Monastery of Dionysios? Are you planning to go there?" she asked. "If so be sure to follow the track down to the river. The spring flowers are unbelievable this year."

"You don't know by any chance why the monastery was dedicated to Agios Dionysios?" I asked.

"Do you know, dear? Do you know why the monastery is dedicated to Dionysios?"

"No idea," the Oyster replied. He threw me a rueful look, before he clammed back into his shell and shuffled off. His wife looked distracted and apologetic.

"You must forgive us - my husband has an appointment with the curator of the museum. Are you here to climb the mountain?" she asked.

"We came down yesterday. Hence the - " and I flexed my stiff legs to demonstrate my inability to climb anywhere again.

"I know what it's like. Well, I wish you a happy trip today. Goodbye." Her farewell was courteous and final, like one long used to dismissing those who dared to invade without appointment the silent world of academia.

"Did I hear the word 'monastery'?" said a lively voice behind me. "Can we offer you a lift? We're going there right now." I turned to find a vivacious American woman behind me. It was an opportunity too good to be missed.

The weather was surprisingly fine as we drove deep into the Mt. Olympus massif. It seemed strange that we had been in the refuge-hut high in the mountain less than twenty-four hours earlier. The couple were in their early forties, the woman lively and irrepressible, her husband calm and placid. As he manoeuvred the pot-holes in the road, his wife began to paint her nails scarlet - "not for the gaads up there, honey, but to stop my goddam nails from splitting. Haaaah!" She had a laugh that was more of a scream. A sparkling eye looked briefly back at us around the neck-rest.

I told them how the weather had been against us when we'd climbed the mountain.

"We were in the mountain two days ago," said the American woman. "My dearly beloved here pushed on up alone, but got himself into a blizzard. Boy, was I glad to see him down again!" She put a playful hand to her husband's arm. "I was glad to see you again, honey! D'you hear that?"

The sparkling eye once more looked around the neck-rest. "That's some man you have here, honey. I couldn't get mine anywhere the day after we'd come down the mountain. You hear that, Harry? You're a goddam hero! Haaaaah!" I wondered why I wasn't a goddam heroine but let it pass.

"Do I turn down here?" asked her level-headed husband. We had come to a fork in the road. We consulted a map and decided it was the way. One last hairpin bend and we came to a clearing. Here the grey stone Monastery of Agios Dionysios glinted in the sunlight against a backdrop of pine-clad mountain peaks soaring to a deep blue sky. Into such pine forests the women worshippers of the god Dionysos had once come in a state of ecstatic frenzy. I hadn't yet told Harry we were going on to see the last vestiges of such Dionysiac worship which I knew existed, knowing how he would turn tail at the idea.

We went through a high, arched entranceway to a weedy courtyard with ruined walls. The monastery had been bombed by the Germans in the last war because they suspected the monks of harbouring the resistance; before then the church had been renowned for its frescoes.

We were met by a solitary monk, an elderly rheumy-eyed fellow with thin grey hair and a wispy beard. I asked if we could look around and he inclined his head and gestured to us to cross to the only building still standing. This we learned was the old refectory. It was sparsely furnished with a few faded frescoes. High up the walls were pointed arched windows with no glass to them, through which the pine forested slopes of Olympus could be glimpsed.

The American woman ranged around the refectory, and finally said: "What a goddam shame! But that's war for you!"

They put money in the offertory and lit two candles. Harry hung back, then thought he had better be seen to give something too, and deposited a few coins.

"So where to now? Did one of you guys say something about a river?" I told them of the track which I knew led to it.

We found the track and worked our way stiffly down to the river below. Everywhere the profusion of flowers was as though a hand had carefully tended a wild herbaceous border, filling every corner with clumps of bright colour. The birds positively wolf-whistled at us from the branches of trees.

Suddenly we were there, with the river before us flowing gently around grey-black boulders. The tranquillity was absolute. Further upstream was a deep rock pool, its clear waters pale green and seamless as glass with nothing more polluting to them than the shadows cast from overhanging ferns and grasses, and shafts of sunlight dappling the pebbles of the river-bed. Beyond, the mountain soared upwards to the blue sky. It was to just such a place that goddesses might come from the trees to bathe naked with their attendants.

"Oh my! isn't this quite something!" said the American woman. Her husband took out his camera and leapt from boulder to boulder, taking photographs from different angles. We eased ourselves painfully down to sitting positions on the river bank.

"Doesn't it just make you believe in Gaad looking at this!"

"Or in gods?" I suggested.

"Trust you, honey, to be different! Haaaaah!" Her laugh flew around the mountain, bouncing off the rocks and echoing from crevices.

"So who was this Dionysos you were telling us about?" she asked. She had thick dark hair which she sometimes gathered back into a velvet elastic band, and sometimes shook free around her animated face, as though uncertain which way to wear it.

I told her what I knew. According to legend Zeus had fallen for the beautiful mortal woman, Semele. But Hera (the ever jealous wife of Zeus) was so enraged by this love-affair, that she persuaded Semele to ask Zeus to show himself to her in his full glory. The result, as Hera well knew, would be disastrous, as the blaze of Zeus' godship instantly reduced the poor girl to a cinder.

Lord Zeus, however, saved the embryo of his unborn child and, rather oddly, placed it in his thigh until Dionysos was ready to be born.

"Wow! that's some wild story! that's paganism for you!" said the woman. She told us she was a Roman Catholic and saw in everything God's love and grace. "You've only to look at nature to see the hand of Gaad," she said.

"Mightn't nature just be evolution?" I suggested.

"I believe what's written in Genesis, honey. And if you were to ask me, which you haven't - but if you were to, then I'd tell you I believe in Gaad the Father, Gaad the Son and Gaad the Holy Ghost." She must have noticed my expression of amazement that anyone could have such firm convictions, because she said cheerfully: "Well, I guess you're just a poor lost soul, honey! Haaaah!"

"It's gone! You startled the dragon-fly!" Her husband remained transfixed to his boulder with the camera to his eye. But the dragon-fly remained elusive and for a while we all kept silent hoping for its return.

I thought how I would return one day in summer. I felt cheated of achieving my goal of getting up to see the Throne of Zeus. There must be another trail, an easy one, to the Plateau of the Muses where we could stay the night in the Christos Kakalos refuge-hut. It was there that it was believed the gold palaces of the gods had stood. There that the Muses had once danced to the accompaniment of Apollo's lyre, whilst Zeus on his throne looked on with his 'far seeing eye'. His 'far seeing eye' (a roving one) had been in the habit of spotting mortal and immortal beauties by whom he'd fathered children. He'd become father of the Muses by Mnemosyne whose name means 'Memory'.

"The old god Zoo, or whatever he was called, was always having it off with some poor woman or another," Harry had said when I'd put the idea to him of doing the Muse trail one day. "Thank God Christianity came along."

For some reason I found myself defending Zeus. "Well, at least the women were all taken in love. Poor Mary conceived without knowing anything. Can you imagine that?" But we hadn't pursued the subject, it being rather too sacred for a frank discussion.

When we got back to the monastery the rheumy-eyed monk joined us. I told him in Greek that his monastery had been built in a wonderful setting, and asked why it was dedicated to Agios Dionysios? To my question 'who was Agios Dionysios?' he answered that he'd been a holy man. Why, I then asked, had the monastery been built just there? I didn't point out, much as I would have liked to have done, that it had been Dionysos (pagan god) territory. The monk thought for a while, then rested his sad eyes on mine, and said: "The monastery it is here because it is the will of God."

"Ah! The will of God," I said politely, and could think of nothing more to say.

The monk handed around a plate of Turkish delight. Such a simple gesture of hospitality prompted me to take out a note and put it on top of Harry's few coins on the offertory plate. I noticed Harry's eyes widen as I did this, but he smiled and all but fawned whilst in the monk's presence. Once back at our hotel in the privacy of our room, however, he raised the subject.

"Five thousand drachma! Just because he gave us two pence worth of Turkish delight!"

"Oh. It was the first note that came out. I couldn't very well take it back again."

"Of course you could."

"Well, so could you, come to that."

"Hmmm." But he continued on the offensive. "For one who is agnostic you're very ready to give money to a monastery."

"And you, I suppose, are the righteous one, but hang on to every penny?"

"Yes, and quite right. Five thousand! All for a piece of Turkish delight! What on earth made you do it?"

I mulled over the 'why?' then eventually replied: "The will of God?"

Harry snorted. But again, there was really nothing more that could be said.

Soon after there was a knock on the door, and the American woman put her head around. She offered us a gift of two crepe bandages, to wind around Harry's 'goddam legs'. They were leaving Greece and flying on to Paris. "I guess we won't be needing leg supports in Paris, honey."

I went down to see them off and, when we finally said good-bye, the woman looked cheerfully at me as she waved from the car window "Choose to believe, honey! Remember you have that choice!"

"Do you choose what you think?" I queried.

She didn't argue the point, but said: "Oh, Boy! You've that heathen look again! I guess we'll just have to keep you in our prayers. Haaaah!"

Whilst under the shadow of Olympus it was imperative to see the site of the ancient city of Dion. Situated on the flat terrain, between the foot of Mt. Olympus and the sea, Dion had once been the site where Alexander the Great had trained his troops and had sacrificed to Zeus, before setting out on his military campaigns to conquer the world. Looming in the distance, veiled by a gossamer haze, was the mountain, its upper reaches streaked with crevices of snow, its peaks hidden in cloud.

An ancient Greek theatre lay a little way from the main archaeological site, constructed around a man-made embankment. It was possibly at this theatre that Euripides' drama The Bacchae had its first performance. The play is highly charged with emotion, and portrays the fate of those who scorn or who deny a god.

'Mortals who dare belittle things divine!
Ah, but the Gods in subtle ambush wait:
On treads the foot of time; - '

In the play terrible things are the consequence of lack of belief, and the king (who scoffs at the claim of Dionysos that he is a god, and believes only in his own strength and authority) becomes the victim, and is destroyed brutally by the power of the god he scorns. It is good threatening stuff, and a warning to all sceptics.

"You can make anything happen in a play," came the dismissive reply from Harry, when I told him of the power of Dionysos in it. To Harry Dionysos was small fry - a mere nonentity.

The Bacchae was believed to have been written as the result of Euripides having had a last minute conversion, which I supposed showed there was hope for everyone even to the last gasp.

The vast periphery of Dion was too much to hobble around in our present stiff state. Harry began to mutiny and decided to wait for me at the cafeteria, whilst I limited myself to seeing an early Christian basilica, which I'd read had been built over the old temple of Zeus. According to one source it had been dedicated to Agios Pareskevi (Holy Preparation), a suitable dedication for a church hoping to draw pagans into the Christian fold.

I found its cruciform outline. So here in the shadow of Olympus, as early as the fourth century, Christians had chanted their Byzantine hymns. No doubt Christianity wouldn't have been so strange to the locals who were accustomed to the Orphic mysteries. The second century traveller, Pausanius, wrote of Orpheus as having 'obtained great power because people believed he discovered divine mysteries, rites to purify wicked actions, cures for diseases, defences against the curses of heaven...', which I thought sounded quite Gospel-like.

"Orpheus as in the opera 'Orpheus'?" queried Harry, when I mentioned this to him later. "The 'Orpheus and Euridice' Orpheus?"

I assured him Orpheus wasn't just a character in an opera. He was a real man, rather like Jesus, with divine powers. He lived in Thrace, a region in north-east Greece. "In fact," I said, "he was the son of one of the Muses and possibly Apollo, and was renowned for his singing - unlike Jesus," I added.

"Do you remember that tenor in Gluck's opera?"

"Forget the opera! Orpheus was able to work miracles!"

"He might have worked miracles but he couldn't save his wife," came the dismissive response from one quite unconcerned about the divinity, and only interested in the opera.

As I returned to the main stone-slabbed ancient street, I saw an elderly couple walking in single file and slowly approaching. The woman was soon unmistakable in her jeans and cotton blouse, with her short white hair swept up and back from a face etched with caution and anxiety. Her husband looked like part of the depressing excavations, as though he had recently been uncovered from the devastations of an earthquake. He had a camera around his neck and wore a battered panama.

They were about ten yards away, when he turned at his wife's bidding. After a few words with her, he looked in my direction and his wife came forward with a spontaneous smile.

"We were hoping we might meet again," she said. "My husband made enquiries on your behalf about the Monastery of Dionysios. Tell her, dear."

Peering out from his crusty shell, the Oyster said: "They tell me it was built in the fifteenth century by the Abbot Dionysios. He was originally abbot of the Philotheou Monastery on the Holy Mountain - you have, of course, heard of Mt. Athos? I am told that after some dissensions broke out there the monk left Athos and founded the monastery on Mt. Olympus."

"How very kind of you to enquire," I said. "Yes, we're hoping to go on to see the Holy Mountain."

"My husband never likes questions to remain unanswered, do you, dear?"

The Oyster made no comment, gave a brief nod in my direction, raised his hat, and continued on his way. His wife

smiled distractedly, paused just long enough to say she hoped
I'd enjoy the rest of my journey, then hurried after him.

That evening I was drawn out onto the balcony to our
hotel bedroom by the low melodious tinkling of bells which
came intermittently from across the river. Through the
trees I glimpsed a train of mules following their muleteer
up a track. One or two had saddle-bags, most were bare-
backed. A movement made me look around and I saw in
the shadows the Oyster seated on his balcony smoking a
pipe and reading a book. In a moment the Oyster's wife
had come out also. She caught sight of me.

"Good evening again!"

I pointed out the animals through the trees. "The
refuge-hut up Mt. Olympus gets its provisions once a
week carried up by mule," I said. "I expect they're being
prepared for an early start tomorrow."

She leaned on the balcony, her brushed up white hair
giving her an air of energy and purpose. Eventually she
said: "By the way, we've been giving your question more
thought regarding the monastery on Mt. Olympus." She
turned to her husband. "Tell her, dear. Tell her what we've
been discussing."

The Oyster peered across at me from his crusty shell.
I glimpsed the slightest sign of interest shining like a star
- like a pearl, perhaps - from the depths of academia.

"I assume the early Christians sought to disarm the
popular tradition of local worship by dedications of holy
places to Christian saints with names similar to the old
gods," he answered. "In this manner they would in time
render what they termed evil demons as forces for good

under the sign of the cross."

"That's what I suspected," I answered.

"I don't know if you are aware that in a small town called Elassona a few miles south of here, there is an early Byzantine church dedicated to Panagia Olympiotissa? The literal translation would be the 'All Holy Olympian Woman'."

"Really? How interesting."

He drew on his pipe a moment, then went on: "And you know, of course, that in Athens the Daphni Monastery's earliest basilica church was built in the fifth century on the site of the old temple of Daphneos Apollo?"

"Was it really? And we never went there!"

"You were saying, dear, that the god Dionyos was worshipped on this mountain."

"That might well have been a contributing factor to the monastery's dedication," he agreed. He pondered the matter with his pipe for a moment, then went on: "It occurs to me that nothing changes, only human perceptions with the help of language. That's the best I can do for you without access to further material on the subject."

The crusty old Oyster's face changed expression a fraction as the morose mouth gathered into a humorous pucker, and the drooping lids lifted a fraction revealing a twinkle in the eye. He got up from his seat. "Well, it's getting cold, I'm going in, dear," he said to his wife. Then, with a brief nod in my direction and the final suspicion of a smile, he picked up his book and returned to his room with his wife following closely on his heels.

After a while Harry came hobbling out carrying a bag of peanuts, two glasses and a bottle of wine. I told him about my newly acquired knowledge regarding the Church of Panagia Olympiotissa.

"The All Holy Olympian Woman! Isn't that fascinating?" I remarked. "Of all dedications here in the vicinity of Mt. Olympus, to have a church dedicated to the All Holy Olympian Woman!"

But Harry wasn't into such musings and talked instead about a bullock that jumped gates and how he feared by now his whole herd might have got out. He poured out the wine and handed me a glass. "And it's another week before we're home again!"

I thought how in another week I'd probably be chasing bullocks. I preferred being where I was with a glass of wine. That the women worshippers of Dionysos in antiquity had gone wild with ecstasy and chased bullocks as part of the ritual, tearing them apart with their bare hands and devouring the flesh was very peculiar. The more peculiar because I'd never managed to catch a bullock in my life. But many things in religion were peculiar.

As we sat out on the balcony sipping wine, the melodious tinkling of bells grew fainter. The sky slowly turned vermilion, then gradually darkened to a colourwash of indigo blue. The bulk of Olympus loomed against the skyline, filtering down to us the legends and stories of antiquity. The mysteries of the unknown continued to haunt me as the evening light darkened, then enfolded in a steely black outline, the awesome and eternal mountain of the gods.

LANGADHÁS

"Why are we here?" Harry asked. "This can't be Mt. Athos?"

We had just arrived in flat terrain at the small town of Langadhás about fifteen kilometres north of Thessaloniki. Frequent mentions of Mt. Athos had been my cover for the Anestenaria festival which was more or less on the way - well, considerably out of the way, in fact - but Harry was not to know.

When I told Harry the truth the result was less disastrous than I'd expected. He began to unpack his haversack with the words 'God help us!'

I distracted his attention by pointing out a stork standing patiently in a round, straggly construction of twigs on the top of a telegraph pole a few metres down the road from our hotel balcony. Tiny heads bobbed up from the depths of this ragged round basket of a nest. The mother stood aloof in the afternoon sun and ignored the beseeching beaks.

It was the 20th May, the eve of the feast-day of

St. Constantine (alias Constantine the Great) and his mother Helena. Here in Langadhás the Anastenarides (a brotherhood believing themselves especially chosen by Constantine) dance before his icons invoking the saint (alias emperor) until, in a state of ecstasy they are able to perform fire-walking feats.

My interest was that it was believed to be a surviving custom from the worship of the old god Dionysos. Constantine, whilst being the first emperor to recognize Christianity as a true religion and giving it a leg up into the religious saddle, had also tolerated the customary homage and sacrifice given to the Olympian deities.

That evening we set out for the Konaki, a room used for the activities of the Anastenarides. I finally located the building set back from the road on the outskirts of the town. It had a dirt track to it and a wide sandy area both in front and alongside.

There were few people there and Harry, who was by now thoroughly suspicious, remained standing near the door with a my-wife's-out-of-control sort of look on his face. I sat down on a bench along one wall beside a portly middle-aged man in an open-necked shirt. He looked relaxed but had a certain air of authority as he sat with a hand on each knee surveying the people coming in.

I asked him whether we could stay and watch and whether we could take photographs, and he seemed quite happy to allow us to do both. Soon a gypsy looking individual arrived, shook hands with him and kissed his hand and I realized immediately that my portly neighbour must be the Chief. Was he the Archianastenaris, I asked? Yes, he was, he replied affably. I felt suitably put in my place and wondered whether I should kiss his hand too but, instead, retreated a little from his august presence to allow others of the brotherhood to come near him.

We eventually sat on the opposite side of the room where Harry began to whisper that we were obviously intruding into a private celebration. I told him it was quite in order to be there but Harry persisted, saying that the Chief was only being polite in allowing us to remain and he wanted to leave anyway. I hissed back that to go now would show contempt. Then I added that if he didn't keep quiet St. Constantine would get a hold of him as he had these people. Harry whispered: "St. Constantine? Who the hell is he?"

"The Great."

"Constantine the Great? I didn't know he was a saint?"

"Well, now you know."

Another couple entered furtively and sat shyly down. They too were foreign tourists which helped to relieve Harry's feelings of being the only intruder but also added to his awareness that he was amongst way-out people. The woman looked like a hippy with flowing hair and a long printed skirt and sandals; the man was good-looking with an effeminate face, longish curls which fell endearingly over his forehead and around his ears, and a dreamy far-away expression. We formed a small clique with our cameras and in due course we learned that he was from Australia and was making an academic study of music and its ability to induce trance. Foolishly this prompted me to joke to Harry that he might fall into a trance but he wouldn't know it and would start dancing with an icon. He wasn't amused.

Along the far wall of the Konaki was a table covered with a white cloth. On it were placed the icons (some of great age) of Constantine and Helena his mother. The icons possessed divine power in the eyes of the Anastenarides.

Dancing before them was the way they laid themselves open to their supernatural energy. Placed at one end of the icon table was a pile of large red silk kerchiefs embroidered with gold. These were the Amanetia which were sacred objects brought out only for festive occasions.

The Anastenarides are Christian but the Orthodox Church frowns on them. Despite the Church's disapproval, as a group they are known to do good, to perform miracles and to give to the poor and relieve suffering. For long they were disowned by the Church but later, when their strange customs persisted and would not go away, the Church housed their icons for them and, until recently, the priest sanctified matters by being present at the sacrifice of the bull.

The squealing drone of a bagpipe tuning up was heard and a moment later a middle-aged stocky individual came in with a goat-skin bagpipe under one arm. A strong, well-built young bearded man in a check shirt began to beat a repetitive rhythm on the sacred drum - boom-boom, te-boom. A young boy seated himself nearby and joined in with a lyre which he played with a bow.

A moustached, skinny character began to dance, arms to one side then to the other as he went forward and back before the icons. He wore a bright shirt, jeans and no shoes, only socks. A second man joined him wearing shoes, and then a well-endowed girl in green skirt and gym-shoes. Their strange dancing was performed keeping their feet more or less flat to the ground, hands outstretched parallel to the ground. After a while the musicians burst into song which in turn inspired the dancers to put more energy into their movements as they invoked the icons. Many of these icons were framed in embossed silver frames and strung with silver bells looped across the lower part - bells are supposed to repel evil.

Harry found it embarrassing being there and sat restlessly. He kept drawing breath to say something only to relapse into silence. Finally, I said: "If you really want to go you can." This kept him glued to his seat a few minutes longer. Then he hissed: "This isn't you at all you know!"

"I do know. But I want to see what isn't me."

"Well, I find it very odd." He patted his zip shoulder bag and whispered that he had Mrs. Thatcher in it (a biography) and would get on with her outside. Then rising as inconspicuously as possible (which was as conspicuous as could be) he went away on tiptoe.

Boom-boom, te-boom. The girl now had a hand to the base of her spine, palm outwards, and the other palm up towards the icons. The Chief stood by the table and at an appropriate moment handed her an icon to dance with. I had been led to understand that as the dancers came under the power of the icons they would go into a trance. Watching them they seemed to be in full possession of their senses, possibly hoping to go into ecstasy but failing to do so. It was believed that it was up to the saint - nothing could be forced by the will of the individual. I hoped my presence as a wary sceptic wouldn't cause the whole celebration to abort, or that I would be asked to leave in order to give the saint and the dancers a chance.

The Australian turned towards me with an amused, aloof expression. "So what's your reason for being here?" he enquired conversationally.

I could think of no good reason which I liked to admit to. I could hardly tell him that in my opinion if the word 'immortal' meant anything then the old gods still lurked around and I had come in search of them. Or that I was thinking of writing a book about various traces of paganism which could be found in Christianity. I explained I hoped to write a book about the Anestenaria festival.

"You a writer?"

"Well, I write." Somehow to be a 'writer' seemed to overstate the matter. "And you?" I asked

And he told me more about the thesis he was working on regarding music, miracles and trance.

"My name's Jack," he went on. "How do." And he gave me a limp handshake. "My friend here –." His hippy girl leaned forward, her long hair hanging across her face so that she had to sweep it back. "She takes the photos. We work together. We want to know how you heard about these people here?"

I told him of a book I had read - a book he'd never heard of which made me feel quite scholarly, but I was unable to remember the title which was less impressive. He gave me his address and I promised to send him details of the book. He in his turn said he would send me his thesis when he had completed it. I hoped Harry would never discover this correspondence or he would really think I'd 'lost it'.

Only the well-endowed girl was still dancing, holding aloft her icon, her long hair swinging from side to side. A woman wiped the face of the player of the bagpipes with a small towel; it was getting increasingly hot and stuffy. At last the girl stopped dancing, kissed her icon and handed it back to the Chief who signed to the musicians to stop. I was glad to get out of the Konaki. By now I no longer feared being sucked into this brotherhood against my will which I'd read sometimes happened with new-comers. Had I lived in pre-Christian times I couldn't see myself attending the worship of the god Dionysos and going mad with ecstasy.

Outside in the cool of the evening men sat idly chatting as Greek men do. I found Harry in a hornet's nest of them with Mrs. Thatcher's frowning face on the front cover of the book the focus of attention. Beaming rustic faces were wise-cracking: 'Mrs. Tatzer! Tee-hee-hee!' Harry, who as usual never speaks to foreigners, was smiling politely as the book was handed around from one gnarled hand to another. He saw me approaching. "Ah, here you are! Tell them in Greek I want my book back."

In due course the book was retrieved amidst quips of 'iron lady, tee-hee!' and 'she use handbag - so!' and a fist took a swipe at an invisible foe.

I asked in Greek what would happen the following day and was answered in quick bursts of information which sounded like machine-gun fire. A couple of children came up to help interpret but at that moment the drummer came out of the Konaki and I was handed over to him. He was their father and spoke fluent English.

He was, he told me, a teacher from Thessaloniki and had learned English in America where he had studied for a year. I was surprised how such a person could have become drawn into the Anastenarian brotherhood. What did I want to know, he enquired?

Where, I asked him, would the bull be sacrificed the next day? Here, beside the Konaki, he told me. What would happen to the bull afterwards? It would be skinned and the meat cut up for the feasting in the Konaki, and also distributed to certain needy families, he answered

I became more bold with my questions, ignoring Harry who was poking me in the back. "How was it you became an Anastenaris?" I asked.

The drummer did not appear in the least disconcerted. "I was trained as a musician," he replied, "and I knew the bagpipe player here. I had heard of the Anastenarides long ago and one day I came to watch. Then I asked my friend if I could play the sacred drum and it started from there. I became an Anastenaris because I felt deep inside me that there was a spirituality which came from ancient times. For five years I have been a member and I find great joy in feeling I am continuing with an ancient custom."

I said we would be there tomorrow and, with much smiling and bowing and 'kalenichtas' to the old men, we finally left with Mrs. Thatcher safely back in Harry's bag.

"They're mad!" said Harry as we walked back to the hotel, passing a small visiting fun-fair with stalls and merry-go-round and a contraption for thrilling participants by flinging them around in model aeroplanes. I thought how odd the human world was in comparison with, well, with the world of storks, for example. The tall figure of the mother stork still stood sentry over her nest, a dark silhouette against the night sky requiring no entertainment to enliven her. Perhaps humans were her amusement?

Next morning Harry said he would sit on the balcony and get on with his book whilst I went off to watch the loonies and weirdoes. I promised to be back by lunch time.

As it was the feast-day of Sts. Constantine and Helena I went first to the church dedicated to them both. It was on the periphery of Langadhás and surrounded by agricultural land. The church was full and I remained outside where the chanting of the priest could be heard relayed from loud speakers to the crowds.

A young girl with a twisted body, leaning on a crutch and supported on the other side by her sister, did the rounds holding out her open palm for charity. She had long golden hair and her face shone with happiness. She wore a T-shirt with the words in English 'Walk don't drive' which suggested black humour of a sort. I watched the twisted figure make its difficult progress through the crowds, tapping her crutch noisily on the pathway.

I wondered if this girl might be the one who had once been brought before the Anastenarides but who had failed to get the miracle cure she had hoped for. The explanation given was that it hadn't been the will of St. Constantine. An American who had been present at the time had had a massive guilt complex, feeling that his own scepticism had come between the saint and the longed-for miracle. Conscience-stricken he had watched the poor cripple leave as she had come.

On my way from the church to the Konaki I passed small unhedged fields with their various crops, and some with baled hay. A lorry containing bullocks passed and I tried not to think that one of them might be destined for sacrifice. I was unsure how I would react when I saw the deed, whether I would scream or what. There were certain requirements concerning the bull, or so I'd read: it had to be aged an odd number of years, be unmarked, uncastrated and never to have been placed under a yoke.

It was once claimed that the animal used to be selected at a young age and then was allowed to roam freely and safely in the hills, protected by the saint from wolves. At the appointed time the saint would enlighten it and it would come down of its own accord, charmed by the sound of the sacred drum. The animal would then offer itself voluntarily for sacrifice.

Such was the belief of the older generation of Anastenarides. When I arrived at the Konaki, however,

I found a bull already tethered to a rail at the side of the building, with two lambs tied up beyond. The bull had a red ribbon decorating his horns and forehead. From inside the Konaki came the boom-boom, te-boom of the drum and the squealing drone of the bagpipe.

Another long table covered with a white cloth and bearing the icons was now outside the Konaki. On the ground before it was a large pewter container filled with water. As the bull awaited sacrifice the Chief, wearing around his neck the red Amaneti, performed certain rituals of purification before leading his followers with incense and music to the bull. Returning to the icon table each Anastenaris then washed his face and hair using water from an orange plastic washing-up bowl placed beside the pewter container. After performing these ablutions each threw a coin into the water.

The music stopped.

I went with my camera to the side of the Konaki where the bull and the lambs were tethered. The wretched beast looked at me from under his red ribbons around his forehead. We made eye contact - an exchange of animal-human vision. I saw the calm look of an untroubled bull trusting in humanity; he saw a worried female face full of concern and addled by questions and misgivings. I was the last woman he was to see because a tough looking character in blue baseball cap and apron, with a clutch of weapons hanging at his side approached his head, sharpening a long knife. Two men stood by the bull and I didn't see the knife go in. All I saw was the rear end of the bull fall to the ground with a heavy thud. There was no other sound, no bellowing. A hind leg began to claw the ground feebly before it lay still. I took a photograph and suddenly the vision of the bull's hoof clawing the ground brought a great lump to my throat.

I turned quickly away and tried to smile at those possessed by St. Constantine or descended from worshippers of the pagan god Dionysos who were accustomed to such sacrifice, but tears blinded me.

I hid in the Konaki where I blew my nose and mopped myself up. When eventually the tears stopped I was relieved to see a Greek woman entering who was also wiping her eyes. I was not the only foolish woman feeling hysterical over a be-ribboned bull (symbol of power and fertility) who had been cut off in his prime.

Soon the Anastenarides were back inside and their music was accompanied by masculine voices shouting a chorus. The dancing increased in tempo. They wore the sacred Amaneti and let out odd gasps as they danced, their feet flat to the ground, their hands out parallel to it, or up to the icons, or flat to the back, palm outwards. The well-endowed girl who had danced the previous evening became suddenly half crazed and flung herself about, her hair flying violently around her face. A father figure approached and put a hand on her shoulder. Her hair swung gently again as she held her icon and danced before the other icons on the table with the man's hand calming her. At last I had witnessed an ecstasy and had seen a sacrifice.

Back at the hotel I found Harry on the balcony.

"So how was it?" Harry asked putting down his book, "Did your loonies and weirdoes come up to expectation?"

The stork was still standing in her ragged nest but had now been joined by her spouse. It was good to witness normality and the continuation of life. For a while they stood like statues over their brood. Then Father Stork began his own ritual of looping his long neck over his back and forward again repeatedly (like the looping of a rope) until at last he regurgitated food and deposited bits of rodent and fish before the small heads raised expectantly towards him. I thought it rather disgusting and was glad humans didn't do the same. "I could do with a strong drink," I said.

"Bad as that, was it? I'd better have a strong drink too whilst you tell me."

We went out to a taverna. Across the road in a small shack of a café a number of men were involved in their own celebration to the accompaniment also of a drum, goatskin bagpipe and two small trumpet-like instruments. Several of them, well fortified by drink, began to dance in the middle of the road: solitary figures with hunched shoulders and arms raised like 'Zorba the Greek'. One of the revellers must have been called Kostas (short for Constantine) and was celebrating his name-day with his friends. He would most probably have been in church that day to seek the continued protection of the saint. Any woman named Helena would have done the same. The cheerfulness of this group dancing in the road was refreshing after the strange happenings at the Konaki that morning. After an ouzo I began to forget the clawing hoof of the newly sacrificed bull and felt objective enough to give Harry an account of what had happened.

It was dusk when Harry and I arrived at the Konaki for the fire-walking. We sat inside until all visitors were asked to leave. I was relieved because it was very hot and I had been talking to a Greek woman who had been telling me how in Athens St. Irene had cured her husband of a malignant growth in his throat. 'Irene' means 'peace'. Many Orthodox saints have names, if not similar to a pagan god, then symbolic of some virtue.

The woman was telling me how she'd had great faith in St. Irene and had prayed long and hard to her. Do you understand what I am saying, she kept asking me? Yes, I understand (more or less), I assured her. She spoke slowly in Greek with many gesticulations and pointings to her throat and expressions of wonder, so that I got the gist of this miracle in her life. She told me that they owned a café in Larissa and the complete recovery of her husband had been essential to the success of their business. "You understand what I'm saying?" she enquired yet again. "Yes, yes, I understand," I repeated. The conversation with this woman in the Greek language was leaving me a wreck. I wasn't mentally astute enough to keep up with further miracles which I feared she was only too eager to relate.

Harry had no need to pretend an understanding of anything and sat fanning his face with a page from an old copy of the Times. He was smiling in a contented sort of way, clearly happy that the ordeal of the Anastenaria festival was nearly over.

Outside it was getting dark and a bonfire lit earlier was dying down. It was being stirred around by two men using long sticks. I had been expecting the fire-walkers to run through flames and felt quite disappointed that only hot embers remained.

Crowds were gathering and several young policemen were good-naturedly controlling the throngs, penning us behind wire-netting topped by a strand of barbed wire. The sacred drum-beat could be heard from the Konaki and with it the squealing drone of the bagpipe. The woman beside me told me that this year the gathering was not as big as in previous years. Before they had had about three thousand spectators and a much larger fire, she said. This year they were short of money.

The musicians came out with the Anastenarides, some of whom bore icons whilst others wore the sacred red Amaneti. Boom-boom, te-boom. They circled the bonfire led by the Chief holding a small cup of burning incense and a large lighted church candle.

There were about twenty Anastenarides. Some of them could have been gypsies but there were a few respectable looking citizens. I had read that a professor from the University of Thessaloniki was one of their number and I wondered whether he was the tall grey-headed character with horn-rimmed spectacles.

The Chief and two men stood to one side, each grasping the top of a long candle held at waist level. The Chief had his very close to his portly stomach and I wondered why he didn't burn. Perhaps, being a true Anastenaris he could not 'feel the heat', as they put it.

It was expected and so was no surprise when the first man broke ranks from the ring and crossed the fire. It would have been more spectacular if no one had because the saint had lost his power. The drummer now invigorated his beat to a crescendo of noise as though instilling fresh energy into the occasion. Another man broke from the ring and, holding high his icon, quickly ran across the hot embers. Neither had appeared to me to be in a trance but seemed only determined to do the expected thing. Many in the holy ring wore leather shoes and only a few, those who were to cross the fire, were barefoot and had their trouser-legs rolled up. Several women, one after another, made it across the embers also, sending sparks flying up towards their skirts.

The tall respectable man with horn-rimmed spectacles (the university professor?) crossed to the centre of the hot embers and trampled them, one arm clasping the icon, the other held high triumphantly. He appeared to revel in the contact with the heat and more profoundly involved and in ecstasy. Another ran on as he left and, clasping his icon, spent many seconds in ecstatic contact as though in adoration of this physical encounter, his feet deep in the hot embers. They were, so I had read, trampling evil spirits into the fire in order to encourage the good.

All the while the Chief, who was wearing leather shoes and was clearly not going to take part in the action, looked on benevolently holding his cup of incense and the candle against his stomach whose flame still had not burnt a hole in his shirt or blistered him.

After half an hour the Anastenarides trooped back into the Konaki in order to begin their feast and eat the meat from the sacred bull - symbol of power and strength, and symbolic of the god Dionysos.

As we left Harry remarked, "Bunch of crack-pots!"

"Perhaps we're all crack-pots of a sort but don't know it?" I suggested.

"I don't think that's so somehow," said Harry, self-confidently certain of his own sanity. "But these weirdoes here - well!"

"So you don't believe in the power of St. Constantine?"

"Power of St. Constantine, my foot!"

"You really mustn't scoff, you know."

"I'm not scoffing, I'm just not taken in by these things."

"Or the god Dionysos?"

"Absolute tripe."

I pointed out to Harry that he might, from his standpoint, think the god tripe but, from the point of view of the greatest minds two thousand years ago, he was far from being anything of the sort.

"That was years ago."

"So was the birth of Christ years ago and millions of people take that seriously."

"That's quite different."

"Why?"

"Because - it just is."

We were passing a grizzled old man who called cheerfully, "Mrs. Tatzer! How are you?" We turned and saw a stooping figure waving a stick in greeting. "She very good for Britain! Tee-hee-hee!" He waved his stick again and called: "Sto kalo!" (meaning 'may you go to the good'). I liked this Greek form of farewell.

Harry wanted to know where our next destination was, he would then decide whether we were going 'to the good' or not.

This time I had nothing to conceal and told him that now we really would go to Mt. Athos, the Holy Mountain. And if that wasn't 'going to the good' then I didn't know what was.

4

MT. ATHOS

At the bus station in Thessaloniki all was noise and confusion as people like lottery balls went one way, then the other, returned, fell back to where they'd formerly been, until finally they were settled on a bus and transported to some destination.

As I watched this chaotic scene I noticed a chubby pink-faced man standing nearby selling rings of bread. Before him was a large printed notice in English saying, 'Man does not live by bread alone, but by every word of God'. The words seemed inappropriate as he was trying to sell bread, but they were significant as we were about to set off for Ouranopolis (meaning 'heavenly city'), the small town at the head of the Mt. Athos peninsular.

Several hours later the bus rattled down from the mountain villages and made its way through densely forested lowland to the coast. Here and there were splashes and sometimes great pools of bright yellow broom.

Mt. Athos, the Holy Mountain, also known as 'The Garden of the Mother of God', was believed in antiquity to have been the mountain of the gods before Mt. Olympus became their accepted domain. Legend has it that, during some mighty family quarrel amongst the Olympian gods, a son of Poseidon (god of the sea) hurled a mountain from the mainland at his father and there forever afterwards it lay embedded. To stop this unholy quarrel the territory was made over to Poseidon, and the three-pronged peninsula of Halkidiki (shaped like Poseidon's trident) appeared as if to claim the territory. Afterwards, however, there were such continued rumblings of displeasure from Zeus, that the mountain was finally offered back to him. Thoroughly affronted Poseidon expressed his fury by whipping up frequent and sudden storms around the headland, storms of such unpredictable violence that mariners are wary about making the trip around this point.

From pagan legends there followed Christian ones. It is said that in 54 A.D. the Virgin Mary undertook a journey to visit Lazarus in Cyprus. Veering remarkably off course her boat ended up on the east coast of Athos. When the Virgin stepped ashore all the shrines to the Olympian gods - and there were many, the chief one being to Zeus - crashed to the ground and the voices of the gods confessed aloud that they were false. The Virgin Mary immediately declared Mt. Athos to be hers and set about baptizing all the inhabitants.

Another story states that the Virgin Mary, after Christ's death, asked to be allowed to spread the Gospel and was sent to Athos for that purpose.

Whatever its past legends today this Holy Mountain is isolated from the hurly-burly excesses of modern day society and is an autonomous Orthodox monastic centre where women are forbidden. It is said that the Virgin Mary herself guards the territory jealously against female intruders. In the fifth century Pulcheria, sister and guardian of the emperor Theodosius II, landed at Athos and was immediately turned back by an icon of the Virgin with the words: 'Go no further; in this place there is another Queen than thou.'

The power of the Virgin Mary and her influence on many people cannot be denied. But, then, neither could the power of the old pagan goddesses.

Undaunted by the 'no women' law I thought I could surely take a boat and sail close in along the coast? No, it was forbidden! All boats were required by law to be five hundred metres off-shore, I was informed by the Greek tourist office in London. I could, however, I was told, arrange with a fisherman to sail at a time when a monk would descend to the water's edge for the specific purpose of blessing the passengers in the boat. I rather fancied being blessed by a Mt. Athos monk. Such a blessing would surely carry weight? Would fly across the water, hit me like an arrow and transfix me once and for all in the Christian faith?

Armed with this knowledge and hope I took Harry to the local tourist information office at Ouranopolis. When I explained that I understood passengers sailing by boat could be blessed by a monk, the girl behind the desk laughed out loud. It may have been the case twenty years ago but no longer, she said.

Seeing my disappointment she added kindly: "But you are permitted to walk to the Athos Gate, it is an easy well-marked track. Also there is a cruise boat which sails daily so you can still see the monasteries."

Harry was nonplussed. "Why on earth do you want to be blessed?" he asked.

"A Holy Mountain blessing I think would be rather special," I replied.

"Nothing special about it," said Harry dismissively. "If you want a blessing you can go to any church and ask the priest."

"I don't want any blessing, I want a Mt. Athos one."

"Well, it seems you can't have it, so that's that." Because the girl spoke good English Harry felt he could confide in her. "My wife, once she gets an idea – " and he made a helpless gesture and put on an expression of tolerance, inviting her understanding. "She'll move mountains if she can," he said.

"Holy Mountains in particular," I added, rising to the occasion.

The girl did her best to pour oil on these troubled waters and said kindly: "You can always try a fisherman. But it will be expensive for you." Whereupon Harry seized my arm and I was frog-marched out.

Deprived of my blessing we returned to our hotel which was up the back of the town. As it was only May the young and beautiful girl who ran it had time on her hands to talk about the Holy Mountain. She was in her early thirties and looked as though she should have been surrounded by children with a husband running the hotel; but no, this was her career. She stifled a yawn as we appeared. Life in a hotel can get tedious when visitors are scarce. When stimulated by conversation her whole being came to life and her personality sparkled.

She told me that her brother was a builder and was often employed by the monks on Athos. He had even climbed the highest peak near the headland and had been shown marble ruins which had originally been part of a temple of Athena, daughter of Zeus.

"Are you sure it was Athena and not a temple of Zeus?" I asked.

"No, it was definitely Athena," she said.

I thought of the great virgin goddess and how Homer wrote about her support of those she favoured. She was both virgin and also invoked at times as mother. I felt there must be a link between her and the Virgin Mary who now claimed the mountain.

Our hotel beauty told us that she knew a young man who had become a monk on Athos. It was a pity I wasn't staying longer, she said, because I could have met him on one of his trips to the outside world. He was not somebody who had known no other life than the monastic one, but had studied in America and had had a great future.

I had read somewhere that families considered it an honour when one of them committed himself to the Church, and I asked her whether this had been the case with her friend.

"Look - he has everything and is to be married. How can his family be happy? Now they lose him and will have no daughter-in-law, no grandchildren. There is nobody to care for them when they are old. It is terrible for them. Once he enters the Athos monastery all family connections are cut. This is the rule."

"He was engaged to be married?" I queried. It seemed extraordinary that a young scholar with a fiancée could suddenly break off everything so irrevocably because he had been called by God.

"Look - " she said. She had a disconcerting way of starting her sentences with 'Look' as though I were a bit of an imbecile and needed everything spelt out in detail. "Look - my friend is like all young men until he has this calling. After that everything is different."

"I would love to meet your friend," I said to the girl. Then I had a suspicion that perhaps she had been the jilted fiancée. "It wasn't you, was it?" I asked. The question had come out rather too quickly. Her eyes hesitated a little as they sized me up to see how much she should admit. She smiled a little sadly and replied: "No, I am not the woman he is to marry. Look - he is somebody I have known all my life. Once he has this calling he cannot help himself. He must do what he knows is the will of God. Now he prays for the world. Everybody outside the Holy Mountain he regards as his brother and his sister. The first duty of the monks is to save their own souls, and the next is to save the soul of the world."

That evening we took the path to the Athos Gate. There was an air of isolation as we got further and further from human habitation. The track was at first flanked by cultivated small-holdings, but these gave way to tall pine trees and boulders of rock. We passed the grey stone ruins of an old monastery. There was no longer any sign of habitation.

After a couple of miles we reached a high wire-mesh fence. Two pick-up trucks were parked alongside. Nearby were two large notice-boards, one in Greek and the other in English, warning would-be trespassers that a prison sentence would be arbitrarily imposed on anyone who set foot on the Holy Mountain. A bleak looking grey stone building served as the police look-out and a Greek flag flew from a flag-pole. Beyond the wire fence was a forest of trees, bottle-green, shadowy and sombre in the evening light. I was surprised to see a wide triangular piece of the wire fence cut away so allowing anyone to hop in or out. Perhaps the police had their sights trained on this one tempting gap?

There was no question of us falling into this trap because a strange apparition in a long brown cotton garment and a navy cap pulled around his brow, with a brown weather-beaten hairy face from which hung a long grey beard, stood in the gap with an axe in his hand. It was as if we were on safari and had been fortunate enough to catch sight of a rare species of chimp. Beyond him a pleasant looking young man in shirt and jeans was sitting on a kitchen chair under a pine tree. This encounter was so unexpected it was difficult to know how to behave. It seemed best to keep walking alongside the fence. He watched us curiously for a while then chattered something incomprehensible, to which I politely said 'Kalespera' and Harry nodded in a friendly way. His reaction was to observe our movements carefully, then to leap out and stride to a tree where he whacked and whacked and whacked at the roots with his axe like a demented being.

We walked on beside the perimeter fence down to the sea where we sat on a couple of boulders on the shore right there beside the Holy Mountain. The Eve in me was sorely tempted to swim along and set foot on forbidden territory, or to rise like Aphrodite from the sea to view the inhabitants. But my respect for the powers that be, either divine or judicial, or because Harry was there, or because I'm no swimmer, restrained me.

I told Harry about Robert Curzon who had visited the monasteries in 1834 in search of ancient Byzantine manuscripts. He had gone first to Constantinople armed with a letter of recommendation to the Patriarch, and had felt fully equipped to obtain a permit to this Holy

Mountain as the letter had been from no less a person than the Archbishop of Canterbury. He had a minor setback, however, when the Patriarch looked blank and asked him to explain who this person was as he had never heard of an Archbishop of Canterbury. Where was this Canterbury?

Curzon's book Visits to Monasteries in the Levant records his travels on the Holy Mountain. His quest for priceless manuscripts and his purchase of many had been just in time as the monks (many of them illiterate) had been using them as bait for fishing.

The sea was taking on a metallic colour mixed with the fiery hue of the setting sun. We thought it time to leave. When we passed the gap in the perimeter fence we were glad to find the character with his axe had vanished, as had the pick-up trucks also.

"You could have asked him for a blessing," Harry remarked. "They're all the same these people. They isolate themselves together and become mad as hatters."

"I don't think he was a monk," I said. "Just a worker or something." After a while I said: "You know, for one who goes through the motion of believing you're very dismissive of those who've been 'called'. They would never become monks if they weren't truly devout and convinced of their beliefs. They're not mad as hatters but truly pious people." It was strange how Harry conformed where I didn't, but where I did he seemed to swing to the opposite pole of opinion.

It was a lonely walk back along the track. On either side were tall grasses and wild flowers, and from everywhere the cicadas sang, male and female together. We were glad to come to the first small-holdings and signs of habitation.

Next morning we were early at the quayside and saw many black-gowned and bearded monks waiting to catch the motor-launch back to their Holy Mountain. Far from appearing self-conscious and out of place they were relaxed and totally at ease in the presence of women. They greeted everyone with pleasure and shook hands warmly with acquaintances.

I was impressed by a mule who stood patiently in the back of a pick-up truck, quietly submitting to its fate and destination, without any sign of wanting to leap out. It too was on its way to the Holy Mountain. Being a mule it was allowed where women were forbidden.

The day was fine and warm as we went on board the cruise boat. We took our seats on deck and watched couples come on board. There was an aristocratic looking English couple, the man tall and erect, his wife a pale-faced faded English rose wearing a large straw hat. Unlike well bred aristocrats, however, they appeared thoroughly disgruntled about something and ignored each other, each having a face etched with some down-in-the-mouth grievance.

There were about thirty passengers: several young Germans with strong-limbed girlfriends and, most memorable of all, a couple in their fifties whose features radiated energy and enthusiasm. The man had thick grey hair and a beard and the rugged features of a mountaineer; he wore sandals, long striped shorts, a yellow shirt and had on his head a coarsely stitched battered leather hat. She exuded good health and happiness; she was tall with shiny wavy chestnut-coloured hair, and wore flowery culottes and tennis shoes. Her attention to her husband suggested either that they were newly-weds or that this was his last voyage whilst he was still in good health. As the trip progressed his lean features, although still retaining enthusiasm, looked strained and tired, and I became increasingly curious about them both.

The ship's engines at last throbbed into action and slowly we drew away from the quay. As we sailed from shore we could see the spread of Ouranopolis dominated by its fourteenth century tower, with low hills behind and its pale sandy beaches. The sea was a mixture of turquoise and deep sapphire.

The Athos landscape of heavily wooded hills became monotonously repetitive as we sailed along the coast. Here and there the odd dirt track scarred the deep hues of forest green.

In time we passed an abandoned monastery with a vineyard. During the Turkish occupation these monasteries, richly endowed under the Byzantine emperors, were allowed to continue their Christian worship without interference, so long as they recognized Turkish domination and submitted to it.

Frankish rule by thugs of barons was more of a problem to Orthodoxy because the Orthodox Church regarded Roman Catholicism with the deepest suspicion. The supreme authority of the Pope had never been recognized, added to which a few words inserted into the Creed had thoroughly unbalanced the Orthodox belief that the Holy Spirit 'proceeds from the Father...' alone, and not 'from the Father and from the Son' which came into the Creed in the west around the sixth century.

A voice over the loudspeaker announced: "We come to the first monastery 'Zographou'." The announcements were brief and repeated only once. Anyone truly interested would have already done his homework. Obediently passengers took photographs and raised binoculars. Five hundred metres away we saw the grey stone sprawl of a monastery flanked by tall cypresses and backed by deeply wooded hills. This, according to Curzon, was destroyed by the 'Pope of Rome' and was rebuilt in 1502.

Soon the monastery was out of sight and everyone on board sank into another spell of stupor. More announcements were made at about ten to fifteen minute intervals. We passed a mighty edifice with onion domes (at this distance more the size of shallots) which we were told was the Russian monastery of Agios Panteleimonos. There had for long been a fear of Russia getting too firm a foothold on the peninsula and using it as a convenient access to the Aegean Sea. However, the prayers of the monks on Athos for the soul of the world had so far prevented such a calamity.

With the passage of time as our boat sailed the flat sea I began to understand the extraordinary distances between one monastery and the next, not as a boat sails, but on foot or by mule up and down or around deeply cleft mountain terrain. Robert Curzon described his anxiety on one of his journeys by mule: '...Between our path and the sea there was a succession of narrow valleys and gorges, each one more picturesque than the other. Sometimes we were enclosed by high and dense bushes; sometimes we opened upon forest glades, and every here and there we came upon long and narrow ledges of rock. On one of the narrowest and loftiest of these...my mule stopped short in a place where the path was about a foot wide, and, standing upon three legs, proceeded deliberately to scratch his nose with the fourth...I sat still for fear of making him lose his balance, and waited in very considerable trepidation until the mule had done scratching his nose. I was at the time half inclined to think that he knew he had a heretic upon his back, and had made up his mind to send me and himself smashing down among the distant rocks. If so, however, he thought better of it, and before long, to my great contentment, we came to a place where the road had two sides to it instead of one, and after a ride of five hours we arrived before the tall square tower which frowns over the gateway of the Monastery of Caracella.'

Curzon's five hour journey had been from the Megalo Lavra, the oldest of all the monasteries. It had been there that its founder, Athanasius, had been confronted by the Virgin Mary on a mountain path and instructed by her to smite a rock from which at once a spring had appeared. Perhaps this story accounts for the enormous marble bowl ten feet in diameter, with a fountain in the centre which stands before the entrance to its main church. It is the focus for the Blessing of the Waters at the Epiphany celebrations on the 6th January.

A pointing finger on the end of an extended arm made us all look in that direction. There a small white motor-boat was making slow progress from Daphni, the port of the Holy Mountain, heading in the same direction that we were. Binoculars were raised again and I overheard that there were two or possibly three monks in it. Certainly, had any monk come to the water's edge to bless us, he would at this distance have been invisible and the blessing all but non-existent. Were the monks aware of the interest of us secular lot cruising along with the express purpose of spotting them, as though they were an endangered species? Any creature threatened with extinction is carefully monitored, its environment protected and – well, I was going to say a breeding programme encouraged, but that would never do, not here on Athos.

From the port of Daphni there is a road to Karyes, a town in the centre of the peninsula which is the seat of the monastic government. There they have a post-office and a few shops – but no women. Laymen who have visited this Holy Mountain recount how eerie the place is without the laughter of children or the gossip of women. Isolated as it is, and bereft of the soft female voice or the shrewish tongue, life is unreal. Only the Virgin Mary is allowed into the imagination of the holy fathers as a reality-nonreality in their lives.

Harry opened his eyes and wanted a sandwich. Whilst on holiday he lived his life in obedience to what his body dictated. He began to forage in a knapsack for the required snack. "This is the sort of holiday I like," he remarked. "It's a pity they don't ban women from all ancient sanctuaries and Byzantine churches. Five hundred metres off-limits should be the rule everywhere."

The distinguished Englishman, recognizing a fellow compatriot in Harry, seemed to sympathize and offered Harry his binoculars to look at the skyscraper of a monastery we were approaching, the Simonpetra Monastery. It was perched in an impossibly high spot above a jagged cliff-face. To quote Curzon: 'It was no slight effort of gymnastics to get up to the door, where I was received with many grotesque bows by an ancient porter.' Curzon at first abandoned the climb, then returned to it because his pursuit of valuable manuscripts took precedence over terror.

Harry and the distinguished Englishman were in conversation. The faded English rose under her straw hat joined in plaintively about the heat, her swollen ankles and general discomfort.

I borrowed the binoculars as we approached the great mountain peak, the Holy Mountain, at the end of the peninsula. It was gigantic and menacing, swathed in cloud through which crevices of snow could be glimpsed. Accounts of it are conflicting. One describes it as black marble, another as white marble. What could be glimpsed through the cloud looked dark grey with drifts of snow.

We did not sail beyond this great peak for which the god Poseidon must be blamed. The end of the promontory was a sheer-faced rock in which the first ascetics had once taken up their abode in caves, living their lives in obedience to God, subjugating the flesh in favour of the soul and eating only grass and insects. I wondered how their insides functioned; eating grass must surely cause complications?

The mountain had always had something sacred about it or the pagans would never have built temples and shrines to their gods there. In pagan times temples were only built in places that already had sacred qualities. It was the Christians who selected convenient sites for worship and then sanctified them.

Our boat began to take a wide sweep, turning from the Athos headland and soon we were sailing on our return journey. Any chance of seeing the caves of the fanatical early Christians was gone. We now sailed several hundred metres further off-shore and it was as well to have already taken photographs. There was some excitement as passengers glimpsed the pinnacle of the mountain through the cloud which suddenly parted, like someone drawing aside a mask to reveal his true identity.

"What time is it?" asked the Faded English Rose, and her husband looked at his watch. "One thirty," he said.

"Pardon? I didn't catch what you said, dear?"

"One thirty."

"We should have brought sandwiches. I never thought to ask them to pack us up a picnic lunch." When she received no answer she raised her querulous voice and shouted: "I was just saying we should have brought something with us, dear. We never thought there'd be no refreshments on board. Everybody else has come prepared. Still, when we get back I'm sure the hotel will oblige." She turned to me. "Do you know the Eagle Palace at all? They're very kind. There's nothing they will not do. Mind you it's costly. Still, I mustn't grumble. I'm very lucky really. It's only the heat which makes my ankles swell. What time did you say it was?"

What did it matter what time it was? We were sailing past a landmass which was timeless; here prayers were said at midnight until dawn, and again in the afternoon lasting approximately another three hours, and yet again in the evening.

All this, it must be remembered, was natural to the day's routine which itself was thirteen days out of step with the organised outside world because the mountain community functioned by the old Julian calendar instead of the Gregorian one used by the world at large. Thus its isolation, its holiness and godly inspiration remained eternal and aloof from the rat-race of life beyond.

In due course we rounded the shoulder of land and saw Ouranopolis spread-eagled along the shore-line. We returned to our hotel where we were greeted by our beauty who, as usual, yawned and looked lethargic. She brightened at the prospect of conversation, and I told her how I would now like to see the east coast monasteries. Unfortunately, cruise boats didn't do the trip until later in the season, she told me. But she went to great lengths to make enquiries for us. It transpired that there was a boat leaving at ten-thirty the next morning but, then she learned, it would contain only monks and workmen destined for the mountain so, regretfully, I could not go on it.

A call to a fisherman friend who had a caique and we were informed that he would take us, but only for a sum equivalent to flying back to England. Harry called a halt to my enthusiasm. I must do with imagining these monasteries; I could buy a book or as many postcards as I liked, but I must give up the idea of actually seeing them, he said firmly.

We had a siesta which helped me to adjust to defeat. At about six o'clock I sat out on the balcony and, from over the sea and the forested hills of the Holy Mountain, I heard faintly on the air the tang-tang-tang of the semantron (a long strip of metal which is beaten to call the monks to prayer). A swallow burst into song from a telegraph wire and I wondered whether it had ever had the impudence to build its nest under the eves of a Holy Mountain monastery and hatch eggs. How was it that the human race has developed restrictions and no-go areas needing permits and passports?

That evening we went to a taverna crowded with Greeks and Germans. To my delight we saw the Mountaineer and his wife sitting in a far corner. They were completely taken up with each other and I was more than ever convinced that their trip was a particular celebration, the first few days of their honeymoon, or the last few weeks of a lifetime together. At the end of the meal the waiter presented us with small glasses of ouzo on the house. With that drunk, I nerved myself to go across to the Mountaineer and enquire if they had both enjoyed the trip on the boat that morning.

They were not surprised at my greeting and recognized me as having been a fellow passenger. Harry, who had been hanging back near the doorway waiting to see how things developed, saw that I was invited to sit with them and I waved him over. Chairs were brought and we sat and shared experiences for a while.

They were German and the Mountaineer told us that he had once got a permit to stay on the mountain. "It was not easy," said the Mountaineer. "I had to prove I had genuine reasons for a visit. I had first to apply to the German embassy, then to the Greek embassy and finally to the Athos police. You cannot tell them you want only to come to see their life-style, you must have a legitimate purpose such as religious studies, Byzantine studies and such things."

I was about to ask what field of study his was but his wife spoke first: "My husband was staying on the Holy Mountain at an unfortunate time. Tell them, my darling."

Immediately the Mountaineer related his adventures. He and a companion had specifically chosen to go at a time when they knew they would miss the August celebration of the feast-day of the Assumption of the Virgin Mary, in order to avoid the strictly observed fast leading up to it. Timing it according to the Gregorian calendar, they'd forgotten that the monks there observed the Julian calendar, and were plunged into the one thing they had hoped to avoid.

"So what did you have to eat?" I asked.

"All we had was snake and water to drink," he replied, enjoying the memory.

"And you ate it?" I glanced at Harry. I had wondered if I might persuade him to get a permit for the mountain.

"When you are hungry you eat anything," said the Mountaineer. Some people might, I thought. Had Harry agreed to go he would have taken his own victuals and be damned - or blessed. But he would never have agreed to it in the first place.

"But after the fast, on the feast-day of the Virgin Mary - wow! how we eat and what drinking!" went on the Mountaineer. "The monks they never stop!"

In time I learned that he had been staying at the Dionysiou Monastery and that his purpose had been the frescoes of the Cretan School. We left them, however, still no wiser as to their personal lives. All I had discovered was that they had made the trip on the cruise boat because he had wanted to show his wife where he had been twenty-five years earlier.

It was close on midnight when we returned to our hotel. From the Holy Mountain came again the faint tang-tang-tang of the metal semantron. The moon hung in the sky over the Holy Mountain, lighting the way for the monks who were being called to prayer. Their worship would continue until dawn. There was a certain comfort in the knowledge that while we all slept the soul of the world was being prayed for.

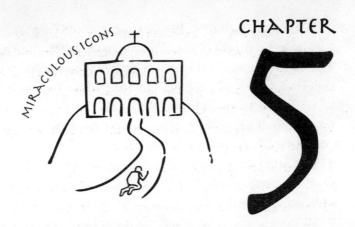

PAROS AND TINOS

We arrived at Paros on the 14th August, the eve of the festival of the Virgin Mary. As Paros was the proud owner of a miracle icon, the island tended to be over-crowded for the occasion and it was important to book accommodation well in advance. I had expected the weather in August to be unbearably hot but, in fact, the meltemi, a persistent north wind, helped to cool things down.

There was something exciting about arriving at an island: rounding a promontory and seeing the stack of white flat-roofed houses behind the port with the occasional domed church visible above them. Tavernas line the sea-front and caiques and small craft bob at their moorings adding colour to the sparkling sea. Barren mountains rear up dotted with the occasional whitewashed chapel or monastery surrounded by tall cypresses.

Paros is famed for its Church of Ekatondapiliani, dating from the fourth century. The name means either that the church has a hundred doors or, as some have suggested, there are a hundred different ways leading to salvation.

The story is that St. Helena, mother of Constantine the Great, (who inspired the Anastenarides with their trances and fire-walking) had been on her way to Jerusalem to find the True Cross when a violent storm had forced her boat to seek shelter in Paros. Whilst there Helena had gone into a small church to pray. There she vowed that if she completed her mission to the Holy Land she would build a large and majestic church on the spot. As she was to die two years later it had been left to Constantine to fulfill his mother's promise.

I asked a plump adolescent at our hotel reception what he could tell me about the celebrations which would begin that evening. He replied loftily that he knew nothing and with some pride said he took no interest in the church and never went. His indifference startled me; but who was I to pass judgement on sceptics?

When we arrived for the Vigil that evening we found ourselves in a large cloistered courtyard with the domed basilica before us. Scattered around the cloisters were marble blocks and column drums, remnants from its pagan past. A tall pine tree was the venue for five church bells whose ropes were being held by a young man who pealed them for the Vigil in bursts of deafening clashes. The evening star glittered in the twilight above the terracotta tiled dome of the Baptistry.

It seemed that all of Paros, even my plump adolescent (briefly glimpsed), came that night to the Church of Ekatondapiliani during the hours of the Vigil: believers, non-believers, non-thinkers and the indifferent, crowded into the church, whilst many sat in the cloistered courtyard in the cool of the night. The scent of jasmine filled the air.

Harry seated himself outside on a marble block and propped himself against a wall where he proceeded to catnap through the night.

Stone steps outside the church gave access to the gallery inside. People went up and came down in a continuous flow. In the gallery I found several families settling down for the night in the hope of a miraculous cure. Most conspicuous amongst them was a young girl in her twenties who had a complexion like white candle grease, who sat cross-legged with her eyes shut in a state of deep meditation. Beside her was another young woman with dark curly hair who was prostrate on her bed-roll for as long as I was up there. A woman with a club-foot came up to the gallery and shook a mound under a coverlet until it emerged. I expected to see someone chronically ill but instead a burly man sat up with his hair on end. Blue plastic supermarket bags containing food and bottles of mineral water, were arrayed beside the invalids or on window-sills.

From the gallery I was able to look down through a haze of incense, past a multiple-armed brass chandelier to where three majestic bishops in glittering Orthodox mitres and several richly clad priests officiated. Everything possible was being done to help bring about a cure for these invalids. I was hoping to see something miraculous take place that night, but didn't like to remain in the gallery for too long for fear of appearing too inquisitive.

Before belief in the Virgin Mary as a divine and compassionate healer, the people of Paros had been accustomed to taking themselves to a nearby Asclepius sanctuary for divine healing. All that remains of the sanctuary today is one small shrine to remind the inhabitants that miracles were once presided over by a pagan god, by Asclepius, son of Apollo.

"Do you know there was a man with no eyes who suddenly had them after spending a night in the great Asclepius sanctuary at Epidaurus?" I remarked, when Harry was awake from a catnap.

"You don't really believe that?"

"Why not? If you believe Christian miracles why not believe miracles that were done before?"

"Christian miracles were witnessed, that's why," said Harry confidently.

"And you suppose the eye miracle and others weren't witnessed?

"Yes. No. Well, they weren't written about."

"You mean because a pagan miracle was never spread around in a Gospel, that makes it suspect?" I demanded. "Or do you just not want to believe that pagan gods were able to work miracles? In fact, there were even raisings-from-the-dead done by the pagan gods. If you give me a moment I might remember who was raised - But, by the time I'd conjured up Alcestis who'd given her life for her husband, and who'd been led back from Hades by Hercules; and Eurydice, the adored wife of Orpheus who was so grief-stricken at her death that the gods arranged for her return, except that Orpheus made an irredeemable blunder and she died again; and had remembered Hippolytus who'd been raised from the dead by Asclepius himself, I turned to my beloved spouse and saw he'd fallen victim to another catnap - I was merely talking to myself, and those seated nearby were smiling at me.

What time would the procession begin, I enquired on several occasions as the evening wore on? Confidently the reply came: nine-thirty - ten-thirty - midnight - . I had little faith in Greek information; experience was teaching me to be cautious. If someone said such-and-such a time, it invariably meant some other time. If somebody tried to be helpful by writing down the name of the ferry-boat we were to travel on, then we should put our trust in the time not the name or, alternatively, in the name not the time. Such things were there for the inconvenience of the traveller but were well meant. If you missed the boat or failed to see the purpose of your visit, well, what did it really matter? Northern Europeans took life too seriously. Promptness was a harassment and not to be encouraged in Greece. Trying to find out the time of the procession I discovered to be a hopeless agitation. It would happen when it happened was all I needed to know.

In fact it was eleven-thirty when the miraculous icon, overlaid with ornate silver, and revealing only the face of the Virgin and Child, was eventually carried from the church. Everyone stood up and crossed himself and stopped munching the bread of Christian fellowship which had been distributed earlier. The majestically clad bishops and priests followed behind this flower bedecked icon as it was paraded with solemn pomp around the cloisters. I had imagined invalids would be waiting for this moment and that the icon would be bowed to left and right over them with miraculous results. But there were no spontaneous happenings.

I had quite forgotten Harry and suddenly saw him still comatose on his marble block. I couldn't reach him in time before the bishops passed and several ecclesiastical eyes dropped their gaze to the sleeping figure. I expected a Pastoral Staff to stretch out and hook him to his feet but, apart from it being noted that he was way beyond praying for the sick, no more attention was paid him.

It was past midnight when we left the Vigil. The queue of people waiting to get into the church to kiss the icon was as wide and as long as ever. It was extraordinary to witness this column of humanity patiently advancing over the course of several hours. The good side of me thought 'what faith!' the bad side thought 'what superstition!' Harry said that it was surely better to have some sort of faith even if a little superstition was picked up along the way. He was a fine one to speak, as he was the first to jump on me when I began touching wood, bowing to the new moon or saluting magpies.

On the feast-day itself the miraculous icon was carried from the Church of Ekatondapiliani to the sea, where prayers were said for those who had died at sea and general blessings sought for the islanders and mariners in particular.

For the occasion no less than five bishops accompanied the icon on its mission. A marine band, smartly turned out in white uniform with gold braiding, together with white uniformed sailors bearing rifles, led the procession with a throng of people following after it.

But Paros is not the only island with a miracle icon. On the island of Tinos there is thought to be an even more miraculous one, certainly it is a much older one, and the following day we were on our way to it.

The sea was very rough and I sat down below and chewed crystallized ginger which I hoped would ward off seasickness. Seated nearby were two Greek women who chattered incessantly, occasionally studding their conversation with 'Ooooooh!' as the boat rose high on a wave and 'Aaaaaah!' as it sank down.

It was when these women fell silent that I eyed them

with misgivings. A moment later one of them left hurriedly. After five minutes the other looked frantic and waved to a young steward collecting rubbish in a black plastic sack but he ignored her. Suddenly she seized a sick-bag and began to retch horribly beside me. I felt I should help by holding her head or the bag but I was no Florence Nightingale. Instead, I put a handkerchief over my nose and turned my back. I noticed a vacant seat some way off and, fearful of hearing the woman retch again, I made for it. It wasn't so easy to get along, as many young backpackers lay full length in the gangway, unaware that I was lurching my way past, grabbing at any solid object, and narrowly missing an outstretched arm or treading heavily on an upturned sleeping face.

Not long afterwards it was announced that Tinos was imminent and Harry came down from pacing the decks to join me. He gave me a wan smile and said nothing but nodded when I asked if he was all right. I made no further comment, fearing the worst. I knew if he was sick I'd be immediately sick also. Early that morning he'd shown symptoms of having the dreaded foreign bug. The hotel on Paros was fully booked and he thought he could make it to Tinos.

Up till now we'd found island-hopping fun. We were learning, though, that you have to be strong; to be in peak condition in order to hold your own in the scrum; to survive being punched in the face by a bulging haversack as a sturdy backpacker turns suddenly to his companion, or keep up the pace as you're forced along by a piece of luggage which hits you in the small of the back. Harry looked as though the smallest haversack would knock him down. We had our own bags to heave about and began using them as weapons.

We went down into the hold to get ready to disembark. It was oppressively hot down there and smelled of engine oil, exhaust fumes and ship's paint. It wasn't a place for anybody already feeling queasy. The boat shuddered as it went hard astern. Harsh light poured in as the ramp was lowered on hydraulics amidst a noisy rattle of chains. As it descended the heat and brightness of the day flooded in.

The ferry-boat disgorged its passengers like a lava-flow from a volcano. Lorries and cars rumbled off with motorbikes weaving their way forward. Harry disappeared in a hurry and, when he returned, found me waiting with a taxi which took us the short distance to our hotel. On the way I caught a fleeting glimpse of the renowned Church of Panagia Evangelistria on the hill behind the port; it was quite different to the domed Byzantine basilica church on Paros.

I had been torn between Paros and Tinos for the 15th August festival; despite all modern wizardry and technology, it is still impossible to be in two places at once. Harry had no idea which island, and I'd settled finally for Paros because there the church was much older. Here on Tinos, however, even greater multitudes of the sick and disabled come hoping for a miracle. Maybe, in the deep recesses of my mind, I'd chosen not to be amongst too many invalids, fearing I might catch some disease and fall ill alongside them. Harry had got a germ anyway but that, we hoped, would soon pass.

Later that afternoon I left Harry with bottled water and pills and went off up the wide road to the famous church. It was an imposing pale yellow and white edifice, with two arcaded levels to which wide balustraded stairways ascended either side. Below its ornate cornice was a row of arched windows. Before Christianity a temple of Dionysos had stood on the hill with an amphitheatre below it.

In the tenth century Saracen pirates had destroyed the earlier church and the icon had been lost. It was rediscovered in 1823 after a nun had had repeated visions of the Virgin Mary who'd commanded her to dig for the lost icon. The nun, Agia Pelagia, had at first said nothing, fearing that she might be hallucinating or it was a visit from the devil. It was not until the third vision, when the Virgin Mary began to be angry, that she found herself fearing the Virgin more than being thought a fool, and reported the matter. When the bishop heard, he immediately ordered digging to begin.

Because the nun had had her vision at the start of the War of Independence and the icon had been recovered a few months later, the icon became identified with Greek freedom and liberation from Turkish rule. Money had poured in from all quarters of Greece and the Orthodox world to help build the new church. No expense had been spared and whenever money had run short, more had miraculously been donated to replenish the coffers.

The custom for those who have had their prayers answered by the Virgin Mary is to make a pilgrimage to Tinos to honour her icon. On their arrival such people show their gratitude and humility by crawling up on hands and knees from the port to the church until they reach the icon inside. Several narrow strips of carpet are laid up the road for the greater comfort of these pilgrims. As I walked up I passed several of them on hands and knees slowly and resolutely approaching their goal in the afternoon sun.

Inside the church was magnificent. The miraculous icon was to the left near the entrance. It was about eighteen inches high and was exquisitely bejewelled and

overlaid with precious stones and strung with large pearls.
The face of the Virgin Mary could barely be seen through
this overlay. It stood on a marble pillared stand adorned
with Madonna lilies. Every now and then an attendant
wiped the glass protecting the icon, polishing away the
many kisses which threatened to smear the glass and
obscure this treasure.

Heavy silver chandeliers hung down amidst dozens of
icon lamps, each with a silver or gold attachment depicting
either a leg, a ship, a house, a child, a cow, a mule, each
representing the gratitude of some pilgrim whose prayers
had been answered. Hundreds of candles of supplication
cast their muted light and reflected off marble, silver, gold
and brass.

I watched a pilgrim come crawling through the
entrance, the grey head down, a handbag an added
encumbrance which had to be swung forward in the right
hand. Those standing in the church made way for her.
When she finally reached the icon she stood up without
any particular show of emotion, made the sign of the cross
and kissed the glass covering the icon three times. This
done she brushed the dust from her hands, tidied her black
dress and went off to light a candle.

A stout young man also came crawling on his last lap
to the church. He was the only man I saw doing this.
The piety of these people and their humility filled me with
curiosity and I began to regret not being on Tinos for the
great 15th August festival. Here was the Mecca, so to
speak, for pilgrims, the sick and the disabled.

Remembering Kuria Alezaki's insistence that icons
should be honoured I too crossed myself in the correct
Orthodox manner and kissed the glass over this treasure,
expecting at the same time a sudden rush of blood to the

head but, feeling no different, I moved on to make way for the next pilgrim.

Before coming out to the Cyclades I had written to the Abbess of the convent where the nun, Agia Pelagia, had had her vision, to ask if they took overnight visitors. In due course I'd received a reply inviting me to telephone when I arrived on the island. Harry had no intention of spending a night anywhere that didn't have its own private bathroom. I left him lying prone on his bed with a hand over his eyes as I continued my bid for holy understanding.

It was late afternoon when I set off by bus for the Kechrovouni Convent. On the way I passed several of the famous Tinian dovecotes, unusual whitewashed buildings whose upper half are intricately decorated like smocking. After twenty minutes climbing steadily into the hills I was put down at the convent set amongst trees. The change in temperature was astonishing; down by the sea the meltemi, the persistent north wind, had been welcomingly cool, up there it was quite cold and I was glad of a jersey.

The nun at the entrance was expecting me and I was directed up stone steps to the Abbess' quarters. There I was shown into a reception room where holy pictures adorned the walls. A young Greek couple was waiting also and I learned from the girl that they had come up for a blessing as they were soon to be married.

The Abbess came in to greet us all. She was plump with a round face and merry brown eyes. She led us through to another room where she presided at the head of a long table. Cakes and glasses of iced water were passed around and the Abbess warned that the cakes were very light and beware, but too late; I had already bitten into one and had blown clouds of glucose onto the table. This the Abbess thought hilarious. She was so youthful and merry that I couldn't believe she was really in charge of this convent.

In my letter I had said I was interested in Orthodoxy and, because of this, the Abbess now invited me to ask questions about it. I could hardly say that I was fascinated by the pagan gods and how Christianity had triumphed, so racked my brains for some suitable question feeling something of a fraud.

I asked her how she had come to convent life and was told that young girls were brought there if for some reason their families were unable to support them. She herself had come at the age of ten and had remained there all her life - she was now forty-six. When such children were taken in they went to the local school and, when they grew up, they could leave the convent and have careers; they were quite free to choose for themselves and no pressure was put on them to become nuns.

The Abbess said that she had recently been to England for a conference and I asked her what she thought of women priests in the Church of England. She replied that if it was God's will then the Holy Spirit would move the Orthodox Church to have them too. I nearly said that I thought it more the will of women that had got them there, just as the will of men had tried to keep them out, or gay wills brought gay marriages and gay offspring, and so on. But I forbore which was probably more sensible, as I doubt my Greek would have been up to it anyway.

After a while the couple left and the Abbess saw them out. I was now at a decided disadvantage as I had no one to consult and with their heads and chins covered I found all round-faced nuns looked identical. When the

Abbess returned and took me off to my guest quarters I didn't recognize her, but thought her to be another nun allocated the job of conducting me there. I enquired about the Abbess and asked what her name was. She must have thought she was dealing with a mentally deficient English woman trying to speak Greek, and getting her verbs and nouns seriously muddled.

The guest quarters consisted of several rooms and I was told that supper would be at eight. Because by now the Abbess thought me a complete imbecile, she repeated this many times to make sure I understood. In fact I knew the Greek for 'supper at eight' but we stood facing each other, repeating the words over and over again, the Abbess with a merry look in her eye, and me trying to reassure her that I knew it wasn't seven, or nine, or any other hour, but eight.

The meal was taken alone in a small anti-room (for fear, perhaps, of what the lunatic might say in front of the other nuns). Before I was allowed to eat, I first had to pause for grace said by the Abbess (I was beginning to recognize her). This took several minutes, but was not so long as the prayers that were to follow. Then I was taken to the reception room where all the lights were switched off, leaving only the dim glow of a single icon lamp. I could just make out the silhouette of the Abbess and a tiny nun about four feet tall standing beside her.

For what seemed like hours I stood with head bowed whilst the two of them alternately recited by heart hundreds of prayers and passages from the Gospels, occasionally crossing themselves. Minute followed minute as I stood with my mind slipping from holiness to the positive fear that I was about to collapse in a dead-faint. The beginning of discipline was being taught; I was being given a lesson in obedience and serve me right for asking if I might stay due to my interest in the Greek Orthodox Church. If I was so interested then I could learn to stand forever as a mark of respect.

When the ordeal was over I was kissed on both cheeks and told to say my prayers before I went to sleep. The morning Liturgy would begin at five a.m., I was told. I knew it would be a long service and courageously I asked if I might come at six. Certainly, was the reply. And could I be allowed to sit, I asked? Of course, was the answer. I felt I should have been chastised, but love was everywhere; no criticism, no judgement, just an apparent joy.

I was shown to my guest quarters by a long-faced nun who lit the way with a torch to make sure the lunatic didn't fall down a steep unguarded flight of stone steps into a cellar. I said goodnight, tried to remember my prayers but got distracted by a telegraph pole outside my bedroom window which had a transformer on it and which, every now and then, crackled and showered out sparks. I worried it might run along the wires and set fire to the building.

In contrast on the wall of my sitting-room was a small oil lamp whose tiny flame sometimes flared uncannily. I could see it through the open bedroom door. I was prepared for it to burst into a vision and wondered what it would be like to be picked out by the Virgin Mary to carry a message to the people. A devastating blow to the equilibrium of ones life, no doubt. Harry would take to the hills if he was suddenly faced with a wife who had been selected by the Virgin Mary for a mission. But, whatever his reaction, I felt I would be a very unwilling deliverer of news from the spiritual world, and could quite understand Pelagia's first instinct not to obey for fear of being thought a fool. Another flare up and fortunately I fell asleep.

The next morning I was dressed and ready when a nun fetched me at six o'clock and took me to the Katholikon (the convent's main church). Candles and a chandelier of crystal drops shed mysterious light on the iconostasis, with its ancient icons in arched recesses, each separated by gilded twisted pillars. Above it a tall crucifix reached to the blue barrel-roof which was painted with gold stars. Frescoes from the New and Old Testament covered the side walls.

I was shown to a seat near the Abbess who sat on a high-backed, highly polished wooden throne. Nuns who came in kissed her hand. A young priest officiated and, whenever he came from the sanctuary, he was led by a nun bearing a candle.

Several times the young priest censed the church and gave me, the visitor, a prolonged censing as though I was an insect to be flitted. I was quite ready to die to this world and keel over into the faith but nothing remarkable happened. My efforts to understand Christianity was making no progress at all. I found it really strange that some people believed implicitly in God and Christ, even believed themselves called by God to serve him, whilst others blundered blindly through a fog of incomprehension and doubts as to his very existence. There was no way of forcing belief, you either had it or you hadn't.

Before leaving the convent, I asked the Abbess if she could show me an icon which I knew the convent possessed. She led me to a glass-fronted cabinet and pointed out a small silver-plated icon in which only the faces of the Virgin and Child were visible. This had formerly been in the possession of a man called Kaniaris, captain of a fire-ship, and hero of the War of Independence. Fire-ships during that war had been very effective against the more cumbersome ships-of-the-line of the Turkish fleet. As ever, a Virgin Mary icon had been a focal point for prayer in those days of war, just as she had been when, in the early days of the Byzantine empire, her icon had been placed on the walls of Constantinople to protect the city; or just as the goddess Athena had defended Athens against the invading barbarians, or had appeared miraculously beside those whom she favoured in times of trouble.

On my way back to the port I shed my jersey as I left the cold of the north wind in the hills and entered the heat down below. I shared a taxi with the tiny nun who had been at prayers with me the night before. She told me she was going down to the dentist because she had toothache. It is odd that one supposes that those who dedicate their lives to God will never suffer from anything so mundane.

Back at the hotel I found Harry standing before a mirror examining the whites of his eyes, pulling down the bottom lids and staring at them. He thought he might have overdone the pills and was now bunged up. Did I think he looked jaundiced, he asked? I said I thought he looked nicely sun-tanned.

As Harry was still feeling groggy I left him nibbling dry biscuits and drinking Lucozade with a tot of brandy - he was a great believer in brandy being a kill or cure remedy, and if he wasn't cured he might as well be killed. I knew this mood of fatalism in him but sympathy, I knew also, made him wallow with the pleasure of being ill; too much attention only complicated matters, so I said I'd leave him to sleep it off as I had more exploring to do.

The sun was hot but the wind cooled me as I walked

along the coast road to the sanctuary of Poseidon and his wife Amphitrite, a Nereid (a beautiful sea-maiden). Rather strangely on Tinos in the years of paganism, it had been Poseidon who'd been accredited with healing powers. He had been known as the 'Doctor of Tinos' whilst his wife, Amphitrite, had been invoked for fertility problems.

At their sanctuary I found a helpful young attendant who identified the various temple ruins for me. He had an odd eye which swivelled around before fixing itself on its object. With his eye at last focused on the foundations of Poseidon's temple, he began to tell me how he hoped tourism wouldn't cause this archaeological site to have hotels built on it. With such a prime location beside the sea he feared one day this might happen. I agreed that that would be a tragedy, and found myself saying in an extraordinarily authoritative manner that, if he ever thought there was a real danger of this occurring, then he must let me know and I would raise the matter with the British Museum. I gave him my address and this pleased him so much, and his swivel eye had such a look of happiness in it, that it was worth playing the part, if briefly, of someone with influence.

From this ancient sacred site I returned up to the church again. I still found the switch from pagan gods to Christian worship strange. Why had it been necessary, and, if not necessary, why had it come about? At the time of Plato the Greeks had believed in a higher, immutable and changeless being they called God who was the supreme deity in the hierarchy of the spiritual world. What had altered? What hadn't was the human need to have a god out there to call upon.

On my way to the church I passed more penitents on hands and knees, making their slow progress up. In a shady area with trees and seats I paused for a while to admire a large bronze sculpture representing a gaunt pilgrim on her knees, with an arm outstretched towards the church.

On this occasion I found doors open to a mausoleum in which a torpedo was exhibited. The torpedo had been responsible for the sinking in 1940 of the Greek cruise ship the Elli. This calamity had happened on August 15th, of all days. That such an outrage could occur on this the Virgin Mary's feast-day and not a miracle, must have been a challenge to belief. But such disasters often urge the faithful to ever more devotion, supposing that it came about from lack of adequate faith in the first instance.

Around the terrace sat several family groups with neatly folded blankets and plastic bags of refreshment. I wondered if they were invalids about to spend the night in the church, but I didn't like to ask. There was a fine line between good health and happiness and ill health with all its consequences. We were fortunate to be without pains in the body, without recurring digestive problems, kidney failure, diabetes - I didn't know how I'd handle a major personal disaster if it did happen. Would I be dignified in misfortune, or would I howl miserably? A few months back Harry had discovered a lump at the top of his leg and I'd immediately jumped to the conclusion he had terminal cancer. I'd foreseen the amputation of his leg, the pushing him about in a wheel-chair, last painful farewells and his funeral. But at no time, whilst imagining these death-bed scenes, had I for a moment supposed that he would rise from the dead and go and live with God. We'd been lucky, as the problem had finally been diagnosed as a benign lump of tissue which he'd thumped off when using a heavy metal bar for banging in fencing stakes.

I visited the grotto where the miraculous icon had

been unearthed, and found it lit by many tall red candles, some as high as two metres, bought from the many booths which sold them on the way up. I then went down into the crypt where there were several large and gleaming copper baptismal fonts fitted with taps and plumbed to the ground.

I was told that a baptism was imminent and I asked if I could stay to watch. Noddings and gestures to sit on a stone ledge a few feet from a font had me at once at the centre of proceedings. Could I take photographs? Yes, of course. In Greece a stranger is an honoured guest, a tradition from ancient times.

A bent and elderly nanny-like woman, with her grey hair in a black hair-net, and wearing a large white apron, stood by to help with the baptismal duties. She had unusually bright blue-green eyes. I later spoke to her and she told me she'd been attending baptisms there for over thirty years.

A man came in with a white suitcase containing the christening garments, which were unpacked and laid out on a ledge in a corner with a large white bath towel. I was told that it was customary for a child to be baptized between the age of six months and a year as it required complete immersion. To do this earlier ran the risk of an infant catching cold, or presumably drowning.

In pagan times children had never had to be baptized to be accepted in the worship of the gods. The gods were freely available to everybody as were temple rituals and festivals. Only certain mystery cults demanded initiation.

A little girl of a year old was carried in on the arm of her godfather who whispered and cooed words of encouragement to her. She was entranced by the candles, icons and the attention of her elders. The child's name was Irene (meaning 'peace') which for the time being suited her.

Two priests arrived and now the godfather was asked questions and made his responses. When these were wrong he was corrected which did not disconcert him at all. He was then given a Bible to kiss and Irene was taken to the corner where she was undressed. She was then wrapped in the bath towel and brought back to the font.

Now began strange incantations from the elder of the two priests who rolled up his sleeves and exuded great energy, and put his hand into the font and flung the water into the air three times, and then appeared to blow and whistle over it, presumably to drive away all evil spirits.

A small bottle of oil was blessed and a little put into the water. Irene, who was by now starkers, was anointed with oil on different parts of the body. This was her Chrismation (the receiving of the child fully into the Church, the equivalent of confirmation in the west). She was next plunged three times into the water, and then re-anointed before being wrapped in the towel and held by her godfather whilst she had a lock of hair cut by the priest who chanted loudly into her face. By now the poor child was yelling with rage and shock. She did not stop until she was taken back to Nanny who helped dress her in her new white satin bonnet and frock. After that she was carried three times around the font. This was followed by the mother kissing the floor three times and the hand of the priest three times.

In this vaulted, whitewashed crypt I sat close to an ancient column which I thought must be part of the old temple of Dionysos which had once stood on the site. I wondered how much pagan ritual had filtered down from the past. In antiquity there had been nymphs of springs, rivers and lakes known as Naiads. The malignant ones had to be exorcised as they sometimes took possession of people forcing them into evil ways. Holy water had always been used as a purifying element, and oil, of course, had been a gift to the people of Athens from the goddess Athena. It was used as a salve for healing and the olive branch had been an emblem of hers, a symbol of victory and peace.

With the baptism over I was given a baptismal cake wrapped in gold paper and was asked if I would take a photograph of the family group. I was not the best person for the job as photography is not one of my most polished accomplishments. But I did what they asked and, using their camera, hoped that I had all of Irene in the picture and not just her bonnet or her feet.

That evening Harry was feeling decidedly better, even hungry, so we went out to a taverna for supper. Seated nearby was a large overweight woman with her back to us. She looked like a tramp with lanky unkempt greyish-blond hair. After we had pored over the menu to decide on a dish which would be the least likely to give us high cholestral, salmonella poisoning, lysteria or any other horror, and the waiter had gone with our orders, she turned and asked us if we were English. I was surprised to see that this 'tramp' had an amiable plump face and very intelligent eyes.

She was Greek but spoke impeccable English and she soon shifted her chair around to talk to us. We learned that she came from Athens and had once lived in New York where she had taught English to foreigners. She told us how she herself suffered from arthritis of the shoulders and knees and hoped one day to be cured by 'Our Lady'.

She then went on to explain how her daughter some years back had developed eczema which had spread all over her body. As the doctors had been unable to cure her, she had finally brought her to Tinos for the feast-day of the Virgin Mary's Assumption.

First she had attended the Vigil with her daughter who had received holy unction from the priest who had spread oil on her hands. They had then spent the night sleeping in the gallery of the church. The next day the girl had had her hands wiped with the holy water from the spring in the crypt. Finally, they had stood in a long column amongst the many other invalids in the middle of the wide road ascending to the church, and the icon had been carried on its gold and silver ciborium and passed over their heads. At lunch that same day she had noticed that her daughter's hands were clear of eczema, as was the rest of her body.

"I cannot explain it, I only know that with the help of Our Lady this is what happened in my own experience," said the woman. "My daughter is now thirty and she has never had a recurrence of the problem." We smiled and nodded, and I was completely won over by her faith and belief in miracles.

After we had left Harry gave me the 'all in the mind' argument, and all the old hesitations and questions regarding faith or lack of it began to rear their heads again. I seemed to be a sort of chameleon, endlessly taking on the colour of whatever setting it was in.

Probably it was time to settle into the colour of faith - not belief as that was impossible - but faith. But then what was the point of faith if you didn't really believe? Harry was no help when I asked him.

"Don't ask me! It's like having faith in pills believing

that they'll do you good."

"All in the mind?" I suggested.

"All in the gut's more like it," he replied instantly, unable to think beyond his recent predicament.

"Taking what's on offer and trusting in its benefits?" I went on, hoping to get some positive feedback from what promised to be a mystical discussion.

But Harry was only interested in the fact that he was feeling better, and not in the minor miracle of it. He wanted to know if we had any chocolate in our room.

Miracles or no miracles I knew I could never settle for faith - at least not whilst I was in good health, not whilst there were more spiritual explorations to be made.

BIRTHPLACE OF APOLLO

DELOS

The meltemi blew strongly, lifting the small boat high on the waves and hurling it down into troughs like a demented elevator. Those who started optimistically on deck were soon drenched by the waves crashing over the bows. Hanging onto rails and girders, we staggered below to the warmth of the cabin. In due course the boat steadied as it gained the lee of the land, and we returned on deck to savour the moment of arrival.

It was the light that first struck me, a brilliance that overlay the tiny island of Delos set in its turquoise and sapphire sea.

"Light?" said Harry, who never had any sense of the mystique. "In the middle of August, in the middle of the day, it's what you'd expect in Greece."

It was the dolphins too, symbol of Apollo. A party of French children pointed fingers and cried out repeatedly, 'Voilá! Voilá! Un dauphin! Un dauphin!' A member of the crew obligingly hung over the bow railings and banged on the hull to encourage these inquisitive creatures to leap from the waves before arching back into the sea's depths. Dark forms could be seen moving swiftly below the surface of the water.

To me the legends of Delos were exciting; they set the mind alight and brought meaning to everything as the boat headed for the ancient port. The white marble of the ruined temples rose against the mushroom-grey of the island.

According to legend the beautiful Leto, an immortal Titaness, had been loved by Zeus and had become pregnant with twins by him. When Hera, wife of Zeus, learned of it she was furious, and forbade the earth to allow Leto to give birth anywhere under the sun. Leto wandered far and wide, searching for a place willing to receive her and risk Hera's wrath. Lord Zeus eventually requested help from his brother Poseidon.

Poseidon told Zeus of this small island which, until then, had been submerged and drifted aimlessly, an island known as A-delos meaning 'invisible'. In response to the call for assistance, Poseidon brought the island to the surface and secured it on four columns of diamonds. A-delos now became Delos ('visible', 'manifest').

The small island, however, was afraid that Hera would take revenge and kick her back under the sea. It was not until Leto swore an oath on the River Styx (the greatest oath possible to be taken by an immortal) that the god to be born would build a temple on her soil and, in consequence, Delos would become the most revered island in the Hellenic world, that Delos agreed to the birth taking place there.

Leto's promise to make Delos famous throughout the world was kept, and for centuries this small island was a centre of pilgrimage. Even today boatloads of enthusiasts come daily, so that the authorities are compelled to ration visitors to a few hours only on the island.

I was helped from the boat by a strong, swarthy seaman, and was very conscious that I was now stepping onto hallowed ground.

"Hallowed ground?" queried Harry when I told him what I thought, "it looks more barren than hallowed."

"How sad for you," I said, "that you can only see a barren island with ruins, whereas by using a bit of imagination you'd see colonnades and temples!"

We decided to separate so that Harry could dawdle at the museum whilst I hurried to the parts of the island I particularly wanted to see. I would then collect him so he could come with me up Mt. Cynthos.

I followed a dusty track and headed for the palm tree which could be seen from the sea. It marked the spot where Apollo had been born. I passed a notice which said 'Temple of Poseidon' and duly noted the four remaining columns which rose against the blue sky. On my way I passed the Terrace of the Lions, large sculpted marble beasts squatting on their haunches, their front legs upright and facing east towards the Sacred Lake and rising sun.

Arriving at the palm tree I found it ringed by a low stone wall. The palm tree was close to the Sacred Lake which was now dry. At the time of Apollo's birth the Sacred Lake had been filled with water, fed by the river Inopeus which flowed down Mt. Cynthos, a low mountain in the south east of the island. Its source was said to have been the Nile, no less.

Leto's confinement had lasted nine days and, as her birth pangs had increased, she'd clung to the palm tree that grew there. Several goddesses had attended Leto but Hera, continuing her fit of jealousy, had kept Eileithyia, goddess of childbirth, hidden in a cloud on Mt. Olympus - not a difficult thing to do in our experience of Olympus.

Eventually Iris, goddess of the rainbow, had been sent to fetch Eileithyia with a bribe of a gold necklace, and they had managed to escape from Hera and get back to Delos in time to help with the immortal birth.

According to Homer's Hymn to Apollo when Apollo was born '...all Delos blossomed with gold, as when a hilltop is heavy with woodland flowers, beholding the child of Zeus and Leto...' He was wrapped in swaddling clothes (like Jesus) which were edged with gold and (unlike Jesus) was fed nectar and ambrosia, the food of the gods. But (unlike Jesus again) the swaddling clothes could not contain Apollo and he burst forth from them crying, "May the harp and the bending bow be my delight, and I shall prophesy to men the unerring will of Zeus."

There was no time to visit the Stadium and Gymnasium in the far north-east of the island. There the Delian Games had been held, said to have been founded by Theseus (an early king of Athens).

Theseus had achieved renown when he'd slain the Minotaur in Crete. At the time Athens had been subjected to a yearly tribute of seven youths and seven maidens, to be paid to the King of Crete, who then fed them to the Minotaur (a monster who was part bull, part man) who was kept in the centre of the famous Labyrinth. Ariadne, the king's daughter, fell in love with Theseus and gave him a ball of golden thread to unwind as he entered the Labyrinth; in this way he was able to follow the thread out again after he'd successfully killed the Minotaur. Theseus then sailed away with Ariadne to the island of Naxos. It was all very romantic stuff until Theseus remembered his royal duties and rather ungallantly abandoned Ariadne

to her fate there. On his way back to Athens it is said
that he called in at Delos to sacrifice to Apollo, bringing
with him a small wooden statue of Aphrodite, goddess of
love, a statue which Ariadne had given him. This statue
Theseus dedicated to Apollo, either because he no longer
cared for Ariadne or, as the kindly second century A.D.
travel-writer, Pausanius, wrote, because he couldn't bear to
be reminded constantly of his love for her. As Theseus
later married Ariadne's sister, Phaedra, it was probably
the former reason. His marriage to Phaedra was to have
disastrous consequences, as she then fell in love with her
step-son, Hippolytus (a son of Theseus by some other
woman) and everybody died unhappily in typical Greek-
tragedy fashion, though whether Ariadne ever had the
satisfaction of knowing this is not known.

I hurried to find Harry at the museum and together we
set off through the archaeological ruins. Apparently, here
on Delos Theseus and his companions had also invented
what was to become known as the Crane dance, a sort of
serpentining movement representing the winding passages
of the Labyrinth. We now seemed to be performing the
same desperate winding action to get out of the maze of
ruined houses, shops, temples as we headed south-east
towards Mt. Cynthos, the highest point on Delos.

On our way we passed less ruined looking sanctuaries
which were in honour of gods imported from Egypt during
the days of the Maçedonian kings in the fourth century
B.C., a temple of Inio, for example, and a temple of Serapis.
Surprisingly there was a temple of Hera too. After all she
had done to obstruct the birth of Apollo I was surprised
she was honoured on this island. Perhaps, though, the
inhabitants felt it prudent to appease her wrathful, jealous
nature.

We began to climb the stepped path up the steep slope of Mt. Cynthos. The meltemi blew relentlessly, cooling the air but battering the senses. Every now and then the full force of it howled around a boulder, and threatened to lift us bodily from the mountain.

Near the summit we managed with care, despite the force of the wind, to sit down on a rock. We were now in the location of a temple of Zeus and another of Athena. Whatever had once been up there was by now mostly blown away with only the odd drum of marble remaining.

It was again the light that most struck me about Delos - a wonderful pure, bright lustre over the mushroom-grey of the island with its marble ruins, domed by the blue sky and 'sea-girt' in shades of turquoise and sapphire. The sea was flecked with white crested waves. Here and there a white cruise liner could be seen sailing in, bringing more visitors, and fulfilling the oath sworn by Leto that the island's former rocky barrenness would turn to riches as a result of the birth of Apollo.

"You know about Theseus?" I asked

"Do I?"

"Well, you know the story of the Minotaur?"

"Oh, that, yes."

"Well, when Theseus set off to Crete to kill the monster, the Athenians vowed that if he was successful, they would annually send a sacred embassy to Delos to give thanks to Apollo. Athens kept her vow but, whilst the ship was gone, no execution of Athenian prisoners was allowed until its return." And I told Harry how Socrates, who'd been condemned to death for corrupting the minds of young men regarding the gods, had had his execution delayed for this reason.

Whilst waiting, Socrates had remained cheerful and

had passed the time in philosophical debate. On hearing that the ship (a trireme rowed with oars along each tier) had just docked, the companions of Socrates had been filled with gloom, knowing that his death was imminent. They'd visited him in gaol for the last time. Socrates, however, had no fear of death and was almost Christ-like as he prepared to sacrifice his life according to the law of the land. Unlike Christ, however, he spent his last hours in philosophical debate, arguing the case for the immortality of the soul. He believed that all things had their opposite - wet and dry, large and small, happiness and sorrow, life and death; and as all opposites were generated from each other, so there could be no life without death or death without life again.

Rather strangely in a pagan world he'd spoken of God (not the gods) and of the will of God. Man, Socrates claimed, was able to know God because each had in himself something akin to the eternal and immortal. The soul, as distinct from the body, was always scolding, ordering, disciplining the body. It was as well to keep the body as pure as possible for the sake of the soul, whose life after death would suffer if, during its lifetime, the body had indulged its whims and desires.

Socrates believed he was, in death, being cured of the tribulations of life and entering into the purity of immortality. Good metaphysical stuff - the soul could perceive and appreciate goodness and beauty and was eternal. In Socrates' view this was not the complete truth, but something close to it, and as near to truth as humans could get. When I told Harry this he remarked:

"Well, there you are! It's impossible for human minds to grasp the truth so, if you're way beyond being able to, don't even try."

Such a dismissal raised my blood pressure. "It'd be really interesting to know what Socrates would have thought of Christianity had it been around in his day," I remarked.

"Hum."

"It's known what the early Christian fathers thought of him. They said that God was using Socrates to prepare the Greek people for Christianity. Hindsight's an incredibly useful tool to prove a point."

Harry held his peace and purposefully looked at his watch. I saw that time was getting on.

With the meltemi relentlessly buffeting us, we came cautiously down Mt. Cynthos, until we were once again amongst the lower ruins. It was difficult to be sensible whilst blundering around and weaving in and out of marble ruins, with one eye on a site-plan being blown about by the meltemi and the other on my watch.

We wound our way between the remains of ancient houses, the House of the Masks and the House of Dolphins, with their wonderful mosaic floors. We then found ourselves at the top of the great amphitheatre. It was impressive with stone-slabbed seats which were not now to be sat on as they had been shaken loose by centuries of natural disasters. A colourful character, a young man in patched baggy trousers, black jacket and straw hat with a long feather sticking out of it, was playing a pipe which was hauntingly beautiful in this setting, and the only entertainment to be enjoyed at this theatre. He looked like a shepherd but had no sheep and, in fact, every now and then, blew a police whistle to warn visitors to keep away from the tiers of unsecured seats.

He stopped his piping as we firmly sat down on a solid block nearby. I asked him in Greek to continue playing, and he went through the usual routine of saying he was only an amateur. But soon he began again and I was enchanted by this attractive character who had been so courteous and who, I suspected, was a student from Athens earning his keep during the vacation.

From the seat looking west we could see the ruins of the Asclepeion (centre of healing on the island) and, beyond it, the Bay of Fourni and the Delos Straits. Seated at the top of this amphitheatre on Delos it was easy to imagine the trireme arriving on its annual mission sailing into the ancient port. The original games, as instituted by Theseus, had in time died out until they'd been reintroduced by the Athenians in 426 B.C. The Delia (the main festival and games) had been held every four years and the Lesser Delia every year.

On the arrival of the sacred ship, those sent on the embassy from Athens would have gone in procession to the temple of Apollo, singing a hymn recounting the story of Leto and the birth of Apollo and his divine sister, Artemis, the virgin goddess of hunting. They intoned chants in honour of Apollo, whilst making a solemn tour of the sanctuary of the god. Afterwards they would have sacrificed to Apollo, and then the games would have begun consisting of athletics, horse-racing, as well as musical contests. The Geranos, or sacred Crane dance, was also performed before the altar of Apollo.

"Three hours on Delos just isn't long enough," I pronounced. "I'd really like to come back one day. Or we could miss the boat back?" I suggested.

"And have to pay for new tickets? And probably be fined as well? No fear!" came the voice of wisdom.

I could see there was no chance of persuading him.

We showed absolutely no spunk when travelling and

kept to whatever rules there were. It was a great bore being so law-abiding.

"Well, we'd better get weaving again," I remarked. "We've still a lot to see."

We continued the Crane dance downwards and north-westwards and came to the House of Dionysos with its wonderful mosaic floor depicting Dionysos seated on a panther. We were in the theatre quarter, with houses and shops set back from a street which led from the theatre to the temple of Apollo. Three well-worn marble steps were all that remained of its great marble gateway with Doric columns. We mounted them and stood briefly on the site of the ancient temple of Apollo.

We just had time to enquire after and find the ruins of a Christian basilica, a fifth century A.D. three-aisled building, with two remaining tiered steps of a synthronon (semi-circular marble seats behind the altar for the bishop and his elders).

"Isn't it odd that the Christian basilica has gone the same way as the pagan temples?" I remarked.

Apparently at the end of the third century there'd been a large Christian community under a bishop here. I supposed they'd wanted to cock a snook at the Olympian gods and throw pagans into a state of religious confusion. For a small island it was surprising that they'd had several churches and even a monastery.

"You'd have thought some wealthy person would have paid for the upkeep of this basilica," I went on.

"You can't expect Christians to set sail in a flotilla of boats every Sunday in order to come to church here," said Harry reasonably. "Once Christianity was established on the mainland they could let these go."

I could see his point. I told him how, though, by

the end of the fifth century A.D., route maps had Delos degraded to A-delos (invisible) again. "Though it was visible enough to be ravaged by pirates," I added.

On the Greek island of Patmos where there is now the great monastery in honour of St. John who was the author of Revelation, it is said that many of the monks there had first come as pirates, but then had seen the light and become monks. It wasn't like that here on Delos, however; here the pirates looted the early churches and sailed away triumphantly as sinners. Pirates in the Aegean had been a perpetual danger as they knew that the treasures of the churches were worth risking their souls for.

There was no time for loitering, no time for the museum. I picked a wild flower as we hurried back down to the boat. The captain of our motor-launch was shading his eyes, watching out for his last two passengers who were by now running along the dusty track towards him.

I mumbled our apologies and stayed on deck to watch the boat draw away from the island. We had all the time in the world now we were sailing away from Delos. The lustre and sparkle of this solitaire gradually disappeared as the deep blue sea began to toss the boat on the white crested waves. The meltemi was relentless. Oooooh! Aaaaah! We staggered to the companionway and went down to the warmth of the cabin, ignoring several passengers who were already looking seasick.

I took out my notebook and began to scribble. I wanted to get my thoughts down before memory faded and the miracle of recalling the few hours spent on Delos sank without trace, and all became A-delos.

'It was the light that first struck me...' I wrote.

7

PATMOS

As the hydrofoil shuddered and skimmed the waves heading for several small islands, we at last saw the one crowned by the great crenellated fortress of the Monastery of St. John the Theologian. Surrounding it was a cluster of whitewashed houses known as Chora. Below the hill was the port of Skala.

At one point the sun's rays threw a rainbow ring onto the glass of our hydrofoil which gave the illusion of a halo around the island. A halo was appropriate as it was on Patmos that the Word of God had come to John the Theologian in a cave, and Revelation, the last book of the New Testament, was written. In it was predicted the imminent end of the world and the coming of Christ to gather up the faithful at the final Day of Judgement. To read Revelation is to be caught up in poetic imagery; to comprehend it is another matter.

At the quayside a number of women stood waiting to catch travellers.

"You want room?" We were approached by a well

dressed young girl in jacket and jeans and high-heeled shoes; she had dark curly hair swept sideways and wore white rimmed sun-glasses. Yes, we wanted a room. She was very ingratiating. To all our questions she answered 'Of course!' and 'no problem!'

She pointed to a smart looking hotel at the far end of Skala. How to get to it? "No problem! I have the car, of course!" The price for her room was so low that we felt there had to be some problem. We were driven to her hotel where we were taken along gleaming corridors and shown into a room with every convenience, including a balcony from which was a view of the monastery.

"You can walk after dark, no problem! It is safe here on Patmos," she told us. "You take the path there and you find the sea. Food? No problem! There by the sea is a taverna."

That evening we followed the track to the sea. On the way we came to a small whitewashed chapel which stood peacefully with its doors open in the twilight, inviting passers-by to enter. In the dark at the back sat a young couple hand in hand, communing silently with the powers that be. These small chapels are a common sight in Greece; families who have the money build them in gratitude for some good fortune, or in memory of a loved one.

We walked down to a bay and stood on the sand and shingle shore watching the wavelets gently caressing it. To one side a long finger of black rock groped its way far into the sea's depth. Patmos was beautiful, a sort of jewel in the Aegean sea, wrought with creeks and coves with the monastery like a precious stone, a dark gleaming pearl, dominating it.

We found the fish taverna and sat at a table on the terrace under a woven canopy of vines. We were the focal point for cats and kittens who disconcertingly sat mewing around us. It was getting dark and a huge luminous ball appeared low on the horizon from behind a cloud. As it was twilight we were for a moment uncertain whether it was the sun setting or the moon rising. In time we saw it was a full harvest moon. As it rose higher, and we fought with the many cats and kittens as to who would first get the fish off our plates, we watched this moon. At one moment it was hidden behind a volcanic streak of cloud but then slowly, slowly the cloud thinned and it reappeared. I said that I thought it looked like an ancient fresco of the Day of Judgement, with the devils of black cloud being scattered as the light triumphed.

Harry was much less imaginative and said it looked more as if we were in for a spell of bad weather.

"I don't like the thought of coming before God to be judged," I said gloomily. "The idea's alarming."

"Nothing alarming about it if you've nothing to feel guilty about," came the reply.

"And you, I suppose, have nothing you wish you'd never done?"

"That's where repentance comes in," said Harry with a certain smugness.

"I've never heard you repent about anything," I said, rising to the occasion.

"I don't go around baring my soul out loud."

"I'm sure," I said, "you'll go straight to heaven, no problem."

But I was less interested in Harry's welfare after death than the historical facts of where we were now whilst alive.

According to archaeological finds and modern scholarship the island had once had on it many pagan temples. The most predominant had been that of the goddess Artemis (twin sister of Apollo and goddess of hunting, sometimes equated with the moon). Her temple had stood spectacularly where the Monastery of John the Theologian now stands. Coincidently, Ephesus, the city from which St. John had been banished, had also been a centre for the worship of Artemis.

Legend had it that the prayers of John on Patmos had brought the columns of a pagan temple - it was said to be a temple of Apollo - tumbling down, killing the priests of Apollo. Such pious tales were useful for helping to win pagans over to the Christian faith through fear. Another claimed that, at the time of John's exile to Patmos, there had been a magician whose name was Kynops. His forté had been the ability to bring back as apparitions to the bereaved those who had drowned at sea. St. John, however, had gone one better and had brought a newly drowned child back to life. That was powerful stuff. As powerful and persuasive had been the occasion when this same magician went wading out to sea to retrieve yet another apparition, but St. John's prayers to the Almighty had caused the poor man to be sucked down and drowned.

It was the limit! a kitten had leapt onto my plate, scattering my food. The waiter apologized and the proprietor's wife came to remove our entourage. She was last seen walking out into the night making high-pitched kitten noises. In an instant our feline friends, recognizing the sound as of a dinner gong, leapt and scampered into the dark after her departing figure.

The next morning we followed an ancient mule track up to the Grotto of St. John, to the cave where the voice of God had been heard. The cave is now incorporated within a monastery halfway up the hill between Skala and Chora. I was as ever pursuing my search for an understanding of the Christian faith and hoping for final enlightenment.

Because we were two lone travellers we were able to ease our way past the crowds of visitors awaiting their turn, each group seemingly surrounded by an invisible chain securing it to a tour guide. There was room only for one conducted tour at a time inside the Grotto.

Squeezing our way in at the back we heard the guide point to where St. John had laid his head, his pen, his hands in prayer; we saw the arm indicate the triple fissure in the rock from which the voice of God had boomed; the three fissures were symbolic of the Trinity, said the guide.

I had come prepared to feel awe and reverence, but my only vision was of human heads, each neck stretched, each ear strained to receive words to fill the mind with credulity.

"Yah-boo?" said Harry when I told him afterwards what I'd thought. "That's really condemning yourself to everlasting hell." But he didn't seem too concerned about it. When later I got indigestion, I thought at once it was the wrath of God teaching me a lesson; but it had gone quite quickly and I tried to compose my mind more suitably to the holiness of the island.

A chance second visit to the Grotto found us there when a service was just over and visitors were pouring out of the cave. As the place emptied we made our way in. Only a few monks and a couple of priests were inside conversing quietly in the Grotto. Candles were lit before the icons and wall-paintings and the polished brass glinted.

We sat in the adjoining chapel of St. Anne. The smell of incense hung in the air. From there we could see the spot where St. John had been with his scribe, the faithful Prochoros, who had written down Revelation at his dictation. I was able to ponder over the Word of God which had poured forth through the triple fissure less than two metres away.

St. John's warning in Revelation against 'the Beast' (the emperor) and 'the Harlot' (the Roman Empire) and 'the great Distress' (God's impending Judgement) must have alarmed pagans who had at the time been faithful to their 'lifeless idols'; if I'd been around then I'd have been scared.

Any such pagan refusing to follow Christ would have been threatened with 'the lake that burns with fire and brimstone, which is the second death.' Before death, though, they could expect to suffer horribly because, after the blowing of trumpets, from 'the shaft of the bottomless pit' would come smoke, 'Then from the smoke...locusts.' To cut a long story short, those who didn't turn to Christ would be tortured with pain, and would regret it for all eternity; those who worshipped the Beast, those who remained pagan would at the time of Judgement be reaped with a great sickle and thrown into the 'great wine-press of the wrath of God...'

Harry said 'not to worry', all such writings were only poetic imagery and shouldn't be taken too seriously. But why was it there in the New Testament if not to be taken seriously? And, if one needn't believe it, was there any reason why one should believe any of it?

We were nearly two thousand years on from when Revelation was first written. At the time, Christ had been imminently expected to come on clouds of glory to gather up the faithful at the end of the world. But the end of the world hadn't come, neither had Christ. So why was it that people were still in awe and wonder at it? It was all very odd.

My musings in the Grotto were suddenly interrupted by a short but magnificent chant, sung by the few monks and priests present. When it was over, one of them took from a silver reliquary a human skull bound with silver bands. With great reverence it was passed around, and each kissed it. I hoped very much that it wouldn't be handed to me as I'd no wish to kiss a skull. Harry looked studiously in the opposite direction. To the monks this skull was a holy relic of a saint and as such deserved the greatest honour. It was this extra perception which we clearly lacked. Where we saw only a skull they saw something infinitely wonderful and powerful.

We left the Grotto to go on up to the monastery. As Harry had predicted, the sky was overcast and the sea was the colour of steel, except for the crashing waves along the coastline sending up high fountains of white spume and spray. The weather forecast was terrible. Harry was agitating about getting away in order to be in time for our flight home. Since it was not for another five days I really thought he was stressing unnecessarily. "Have faith!" I said. But he wasn't convinced.

A bus took us up the coils of road, serpenting up to Chora, to the great Monastery of John the Theologian. As we went higher, the black volcanic looking island spread out below us. Chora was a maze of cobbled, vaulted alleyways and huddled whitewashed houses. The dark fortress walls of the monastery rose from these small prostrate buildings at its feet. It had been founded in 1088 by Osios Christodoulos, a deeply devout monk and ascetic. By diplomacy he'd managed to acquire Patmos in exchange for lands on the island of Cos and had set to work to create what he'd called a 'workshop of virtue'.

We entered this fortress monastery through a small door and found ourselves in a cobbled and whitewashed cloister, with terracotta pots of bright flowers. We approached the main church, but found that a number of monks were rehearsing some chant. As we didn't like to disturb them, we took ourselves to the monastery museum, where I found the one thing I had expressly come to see; it was a marble plaque taken from the temple of Artemis.

The plaque described Patmos as the 'loveliest island of the daughter of Leto (this was Artemis) which came up from the depth as a resting place of her (Leto's) wanderings'. Patmos too, it seemed, had provided a respite for the poor girl in the days before she'd finally given birth to Apollo and Artemis.*

The plaque also mentioned Orestes, son of King Agamemnon, who had sacrificed to Artemis here at her temple in thanks for being rescued from the Furies (winged women who tormented ceaselessly those who'd committed murder). Orestes had been guilty of matricide because he'd avenged his father's death when his mother, Clytemnestra, had murdered him on his return from the Trojan Wars. Orestes had been tried and acquitted in Athens, and the Furies had become well disposed thanks to the wisdom of Athena. It was a nice thought that Orestes had come to the temple of Artemis on Patmos, and had prayed and given thanks to the goddess.

The museum was about to close and we had to leave. The monks by now were gathered in the courtyard, and we were introduced to a Father Bartholomew who was handing out blue plastic bags of grain, the kollyva, the food of the dead. It is symbolic of burial and resurrection and is

* See the chapter on Delos for the story.

handed out at memorial services. In fact, the custom can be traced back to the time of Homer.

The monk told us that, as the next day was the feast-day of Osios Christodoulos, there would be a Vigil in his honour that night and, if we liked, we could come. I said we'd be delighted to, though from the look of Harry's fixed and polite smile I could see I was speaking only for myself.

It was late afternoon and we found ourselves seated in Skala, the port of Patmos, with a young Greek who was very earnest. We had just met this young man in a shipping agency where he had come to our assistance over some misunderstanding with the clerk. Much to Harry's consternation it appeared we were marooned on the island, and no amount of Greek or English on my part could change the situation. I was enjoying the novelty of being stuck on this holy island; but Harry was thinking of money and felt quite unholy.

The young man asked us to join him for a drink. He was a personable and likeable character in his mid-thirties, and soon we learned that his job was in insurance which took him frequently to London. He told us that he was spending a short time on Patmos to help him get over the death of his mother. He went on to say that over the years he had pondered the great religions of the world before finally returning to the Orthodox Church.

He began to speak about the extraordinary phenomenon of consciousness. It was consciousness which made people feel there was an ever greater consciousness, an all-consciousness, which was God, he said. I was a believer at once.

This consciousness of each individual was unique; the individual was unique; no matter what nationality you were, no matter what happened to you in life (or when you died), you would never be anything other than the unique 'You'. That was an amazing thought. I had always been 'Me'? Yes, always and would remain 'Me' throughout eternity, he informed me.

He spoke with such earnestness and belief, it was as if the rest of the world ceased to exist as we sat at the quayside taverna in Skala. He was a thickset, thirty year old, with a lot of body language. Whilst making a point he would raise his shoulders to give emphasis to his words, and bend his arms with clenched fists towards his innermost being.

He told us he hoped and prayed he would soon find a wife and have children; this was his dearest wish. No, he would never - could never - become an Orthodox priest because (and he was slightly abashed at having to confess this, but he did so most charmingly), he had not remained celibate, and to become a priest he would have to admit to this. Then don't confess, I suggested glibly, and he regarded me with sorrow. He could never live with his conscience if he failed to admit to something of such importance.

He went on to tell us about the Orthodox belief of encircling oneself with the protection of Christ by repeating the words 'Kurios Ihsous Xristos eleison me' (Christ Jesus have mercy on me). These words formed a spiritual ring of defence about a person, in the centre of which was the essential 'You'. The words helped to ward off temptation and evil.

I told this young man that I had great admiration for the music in Orthodox churches and loved the Byzantine chant. How was it that all the priests had the ability to chant? Did they receive special training in this? He replied that some training was necessary, but a firm believer would find that his voice came true from within. As he said this, his shoulders rose and he bent his arms with his clenched hands to his breast. What was truly felt within could not come out wrong, he explained.

So much to think about! So much to come to grips with!

Death? At death your soul was taken by St. Michael, he said. You were taken here and there, and were shown the bad things and the good things you had done. What? Big panic! It was best to confess all before death, because to confess all was to receive forgiveness, and you then went to what was called the 'First Rising', which was one step nearer to God.

Fanciful stuff. I was beginning to lose faith again. Why was it that people talked wonderfully at one moment, but then went 'over the top' with their ideas and beliefs? I asked him how he could explain that God had chosen the Jews, but then seemed to have gone on to choose the Gentiles, which rather brutally had confused the issue for the Jews. Without hesitation he said it was because the Jews had got it wrong and were awaiting the anti-Christ, not that he had anything against the Jews, but that was the sad fact of the matter, he said.

I wished people wouldn't go 'over the top'. Any faith I'd had was by now gone.

My earnest companion raised his shoulders and bent his arms with clenched fists to his breast once more, declaring his conviction that a husband and wife were one body and, therefore, would be united in the next world. I looked at Harry who was smiling benignly. Was he happy at the prospect of having me into life everlasting - wasn't one life of me quite enough for him? 'Over the top stuff again', I suspected.

After an hour's discussion of these weighty matters in this all absorbing conversation, the outside world began to break in on us. Our consciousnesses had been briefly united, but now we looked around and saw other tables occupied by those relaxing over beers, teas, Coca Colas. Boats were bobbing at their moorings along the sea-front. The sky was overcast, the sea choppy. A storm was brewing and I could see no ships in harbour. We couldn't get off the island, but it was time to move on.

Harry had a 'who-dun-it' which he thought would be infinitely more exciting than any Vigil and was determined to finish it. I was on a spiritual plain and 'why-God-dun-it' was my constant enquiry, so I took myself off alone up to the monastery for the Vigil.

About twenty monks were gathered for the celebration, with the Abbot seated on a high-backed throne. He was elderly, dignified, with a long white beard which hung down his chest. I was fascinated by the chanting which came as true from within as could be and was never monotonous; there was always contrast to it, as though light and shadow were playing on each other.

I supposed that, even if God didn't exist, all this beauty and music was very elevating, bringing one nearer to men's perception of what God should be. What I didn't like was God's anger and threats of vengeance in the Old Testament. Then for God to send a Son into the world to have him crucified for us mortals, seemed even worse.

Why should I take God seriously? Why, actually, did

I, come to that? God or no God I loved the poetic wonder of the Orthodox Church, and was spiritually 'with it' if mentally 'without it'.

I tried to remain unobtrusive whilst, rather like the family dog wanting the best place before the hearth, crept slowly forward. The church was richly furnished and exquisite. The floor was of inlaid marble and there were several heavy silver, multiple-branched candelabra and silver icon lamps. Its major feature was its magnificent carved and gilded ornate iconostasis with its seventeenth century icons.

I began to notice the key figures at this celebration. There was an extraordinarily handsome young monk with aristocratic features; tall and graceful in his movements as he passed backwards and forwards in a flowing black pleated gown and black cap with veil. His expression never for a moment revealed anything but total dedication to his many tasks. He kissed a gold stole and reverently placed it around the neck of the Abbot, arranging the long white beard over it.

At the left revolving lectern was another young monk with curly lashes, a good strong chin, small beard and determined rosy pink lips. He was the lead chorister of a group of three, and used an index finger to keep time as he moved it from note to note on his open psalter.

I managed to sidle into a seat at the back, the arms of which were carved with griffin heads. From there I watched a monk stand patiently, trying to light the many candles on one of the gigantic hanging silver candelabrum. The highest was many feet from the ground, and the weight of the taper at the end of the extended holder trembled as he strained to hold it steady. The job completed and the numerous candles were a flickering blaze of light. I was looking forward to seeing all the candelabra lit, but soon the one which had been so painstakingly done had all the candles extinguished, before the monk again stood for many minutes lighting another. There must have been some symbolism to all this, or else it was some penance he was having to endure.

A black bat of a monk approached me, and it took only his eye to indicate 'out!'; not a word was needed to persuade me to vacate my seat promptly. He settled himself into it and chanted comfortably behind me.

A book-stand was placed nearby by 'Handsome Aristocrat' and an elderly monk began a reading. He read rapidly in a very precise, high-toned flow, sentence by sentence, following the lines with a finger. I wondered how long it would go on. I still hadn't acquired the art of standing for long stretches at a time when attending an Orthodox service and felt my back was breaking.

An elderly, bushy-bearded monk on the right had his eyes shut, and seemed to be sleeping on his feet like a horse. 'Rapid Reader' suddenly ended his half-hour endurance test but now, oh dear! the monk sleeping on his feet was awake and reading - on and on and on. Fortunately the one, whose eye had ordered me from my seat was himself called away, and I seized the opportunity to sit again.

Meanwhile 'Curly Lashes' had been joined by a jolly middle-aged fellow in an open-necked shirt. He was very relaxed as he followed the prominently placed index finger along the notes in his psalter. The music was similar to the notes of an organ: a low drone, with higher notes accompanying. It was all done with the male voice, of course; there is seldom musical accompaniment in the Orthodox Church.

I could see very little now, except the backs of those

standing before me. I could only glimpse between black gowns a small child running forward in dungarees and staring at the chanters. I was very glad to be sitting because (I stood briefly to see this) 'Rapid Reader' was now in the sanctuary and was chanting the Gospel or something and it was going on for ever. 'Bushy Beard', who was previously asleep on his feet, was now asleep on a seat.

I was quite pleased that a taxi was coming for me at midnight. Meanwhile, high above the altar, there was a small window and the moonlight was so bright it looked as though dawn was breaking. I remembered that the goddess Artemis, on whose temple site this monastery had been built, was identified with the moon. All seemed symbolic tonight.

It was time to leave and I sidled out. In this monastery, where all was ordered and holy I sidled everywhere and was as unobtrusive as possible. As I came from the Katholikon I found an array of solemn faces. These were men and women listening to the relayed service from seats in the arcaded and cobbled courtyard, with its surrounding vaulted passageways, and narrow stone stairways which led to other parts of this great complex.

I came down to the road, and on the way saw fireflies darting about like miniature fireworks. Whilst I waited for the taxi I leaned on a parapet and looked down at the twinkling lights of Skala far below, and the sombre density of several small islands out to sea. The moon was high in the sky but, from a bank of black cloud on the horizon, I saw constant flashes of sheet lightning and occasional forked lightning, and I could hear rumblings of thunder. These forebodings and boomings served as a reminder of God Almighty, whose warnings in Revelation were intended to frighten those who heard them into preparing themselves for the imminent end of the world and, if deserving of it, of life everlasting. Equally, on this island, it was a reminder of Zeus, father of Artemis, who reigned supreme over the heavens, and punished erring humanity with thunderbolts. In the one men went to heaven or to hell, in the other to the Islands of the Blest or to Tartarus. Was there so much difference?

A few days later we were still marooned. Harry was fretting almost to the point of apoplexy. At the various shipping agencies we were witnessing other unfortunates who had been unable to get away having left it too late.

I tried to soothe Harry's anxieties, whilst not betraying my secret enjoyment of being unable to get off this island with which I'd fallen in love.

Marooned as we were we wandered the narrow, vaulted alleyways of Chora, and found small concealed whitewashed churches. We sat in the small plateia and fortified ourselves with food, and exchanged words with other marooned foreigners. Sudden torrential rain caused the alleyways to become small streams, and prompted artists to run for cover clutching their canvases. Athens was having terrible problems with flooding and mud slides, we learned. Nine people had died.

After several days the weather forecast was at last good. It was almost certain we would be able to leave the next morning. That evening we took a stroll up the hill, past the chapel which had been open our first night. We turned right and walked along a promontory, and came suddenly to a stupendous view of the bay and the port of Skala.

The port was a cheerful scene now that the storms

had passed. Fishing boats set out, and there were several motor-launches full of people chugging out of harbour on their way to some celebration, a barbecue perhaps. A rowing-boat set off on some solitary mission; a couple of sailing-boats tacked gently, their sails filled by a light breeze. A speedboat suddenly and noisily scored the water, leaving a white frothy wake; in contrast, black ravens quietly flapped by overhead.

Beyond the landmass, shaped like a slim waist, we could see another bay and stretch of sea. The sun was setting over there. A dark cloud hung midway between the sea and the heavens. As the sun went down, it hid behind the cloud, sending shafts of light seawards. It looked like a vision of paradise. When I told Harry this he said that in his opinion the sooner I got home to normality, and away from this fanciful nonsense the better. "'Red sky at night, shepherd's delight', and thank God for it!" he remarked.

The sun sank below the horizon, leaving the bay beyond the slim waist of land an inky blue, and the black hills suffused in a golden light. The dark veil of cloud above became a fiery red streak - more 'shepherd's delight', I told Harry who said he very much hoped so.

We walked down to the cove where we'd dined our first night. Tonight the sea was tranquil as it lapped the sand and shingle shore. As we walked back up the track, tall craggy rocks were starkly black against the sky. They were like Indian ink silhouettes painted on the finest pale gold silk

It grew dark quickly as we strolled back. Beside the track a number of goats had gathered, standing under a solitary roadside light which shed a warm glow around them. A small owl flew down and perched precariously on the wire stretched taut to hold up the telegraph pole. The owl gave a screech, whereupon a goat snorted contemptuously. A cat came mewing down the track to join us and immediately we had the owl and the pussy-cat scenario.

I realized suddenly that they were all a part of present day consciousness. We were all heading towards the end of our mortal world, and everything we said and did had consequences, setting the example to those following on. It was a sobering thought.

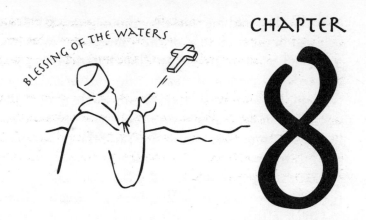

8

PIRAEUS

It was midwinter and I wanted to see the great annual ceremony of the Blessing of the Waters at the port of Athens on the 6th January. I told Harry I wouldn't fly off and leave him if the weather was bad. It was. But somehow the possibility of Harry breaking a leg on the ice whilst feeding his cattle, seemed no real reason for cancelling my flight. I was only going to be away three nights.

If he got the flu, or if I got the flu then, of course, I wouldn't go, I assured him. We swallowed daily doses of cod-liver-oil and multi-vitamin pills, and remained free of winter ailments. But as soon as I left home I inevitably headed straight into the outside world of germs and viruses.

On the plane I found myself seated alongside two young Greek women, one of whom had a beastly cough. When I told them I was flying out to see the Blessing of the Waters at Piraeus (the port of Athens) they were amazed. I was somewhat amazed myself.

Inevitably we talked about the Orthodox Church in

Greece. They told me that they thought few Greeks really believed in the teachings of the Church, but everyone was tied to it because of the many Church festivals and people's name-days linked to the saints. In answer to my remark that in Greece I felt more spiritually aware than in Britain, one of them said that she thought the old temples had been built on natural sacred sites, and the things of nature had left their imprint on Christianity.

As they seemed interested, I launched into what I had read about the origins of Epiphany in Greece. The word in Greek is Theophania. The ancient meaning of the word is 'the appearance of god'. Originally it had applied to a festival held in honour of Apollo.

Legend had it that, after Apollo had slain the Python at Delphi, he had taken himself off to atone for the killing. His return to Delphi eight years later had consequently been marked by the celebration of the Theophania (his reappearance as god). The Theophania festival had been celebrated in his honour from then on.

Today's Theophania is a commemoration of Christ's baptism by John the Baptist. It was after his immersion in the waters of the River Jordan that Christ first manifested himself to the people. Epiphany in the Orthodox Church is of more importance than Christmas. Sceptics might say that it is a sort of annual rain charm performed by the Church, because in the east water is scarce and, therefore, a commodity worthy of solemn ritual.

It was four in the morning on the 5th January that I found myself queuing for a taxi at Athens airport. As I waited, three lusty youths approached the queue holding triangles. They stood together and struck their triangles and, with gusto, sang a raucous rendering of what I supposed was an Epiphany kalanda (a form of carol). The

Greeks in the queue ignored them. Perhaps it was only a drinking song; it was the triangles which made me suppose it was a kalanda. Their words, so far as I could translate, went something like: 'Good morning, good evening, I hope that you are well.' Certainly they were very latenight revellers.

On the morning of the 6th January, the day of Epiphany, I was again up at dawn. A ten minute drive through the deserted streets of Piraeus and I was taken by taxi to the small cove of Stavros. The floodlit church nearby was already holding its early morning service; its doors open to reveal the bright lights of hanging chandeliers, and the many lighted candles of supplication. An arthritic, bowed figure of an aged woman dressed in black, was slowly mounting the steep steps to the church.

I didn't enter this small brightly lit church but, instead, was taken to the cove nearby. It was a small rocky haven, with a lighthouse and a few dinghies and sailing-boats moored in its deep waters. All around colourful bunting fluttered in the breeze.

It was to this small cove that a procession would later wind its way from the church. The priest would come to the water' edge and, after prayers would throw the cross into the sea, whereupon the young braves of the vicinity would dive in to retrieve it. The youth who managed to recover the cross would be considered the lucky one for the year; certainly there was some luck in it, as he then had the right to go around local households to collect money for himself.

I asked my young taxi driver if he had ever dived.

When he was eighteen he had, he answered. Had he retrieved the cross? No, he hadn't. What had it been like diving for it, I asked? Very cold, came the unemotional reply. I had somewhat foolishly supposed the newly blessed waters would have had some sort of miracle consequence, warming the water or purifying it or something.

I would have liked to have remained at the cove to witness the young men diving, but I wanted too to join the throngs at the Great Harbour at Piraeus, the main port of Athens, where the celebrations were performed with especial pomp and ceremony.

A streak of pale red on the horizon indicated dawn was breaking. I was taken to see the different ports and bays which provided shelter and moorings for ships and small craft in Piraeus: the crescent shaped Zea Bay for yachts and hydrofoils with its elegant blocks of residential flats, and with its sunken garden containing a black gun-boat beside the Maritime Museum; and Mikrolimani, the horse-shoe bay, which provided moorings for many sailing-boats and caiques. All were decked out in festive bunting as were the tavernas lining the sea-front.

We drove from Mikrolimani up the Kastella Hill to the chapel on top dedicated to the Profitis Hlias. Chapels of the Profitis Hlias are always to be found on elevated sites. Through the open doors to this chapel I could see a bishop in his glittering domed mitre taking the Liturgy.

From the Kastella Hill in this early morning light I looked across the built up area of Piraeus, to the centre of Athens and the Parthenon some five miles away. Beyond rose the Hymettos mountains, on which were shrines to the old god Zeus - Zeus, god of the sky, sender of rain, the 'cloud gatherer'.

As the sun rose over Athens on this the 6th January, I

thought about the origins of Epiphany. In the early years
of Christianity, as there was no known date for the birth
of Christ, the Orthodox east celebrated Christ's nativity
and baptism together on the 6th January (long thought
to be the day the sun increased in strength). It was not
until the fourth century, when it was reckoned that the
sun's light and strength increased on the 25th December
and not the 6th January, that it became the date selected
by the Christian fathers for Christ's nativity, leaving the
6th January for his baptism only. At that time the 25th
December was the day of a popular pagan festival in Rome
known as Sol Invictus (the Invincible Sun) celebrating
the Nativity of the Sun. St.Augustine advised those who
attended this festival not to honour the sun itself, but to
honour God Almighty, creator of the sun.

I looked out over the houses stacked up the Kastella
Hill towards the Great Harbour of Piraeus. Piraeus is the
hub of the Greek maritime world. From time immemorial
ships have sailed in and out of its harbours. Around the
Great Harbour there are today many banks and commercial
companies which flank the wide streets going down to the
port. The church of Agios Nikolaos (Nikolaos, patron
saint of the sea) stands at one end of the Great Harbour,
whilst at the other end is the Cathedral of Agia Triadha
(Holy Trinity).

The evening before I had explored the area, and had
entered this imposing domed and beautiful cathedral.
Above its portals on either side were mosaic plaques
depicting two colourful peacocks. Inside, the walls were
decorated with frescoes and mosaics. Because it had
been the eve of Epiphany, a red carpet had been laid to
the chancel steps for the government officials and city
dignitaries, who would be attending the service of the

Blessing of the Waters. Before the Royal Doors of the iconostasis there had been a table covered with a white cloth, and on it a large silver urn. Curtains to the doors of the iconostasis were pale blue (symbolic blue for the occasion) as were the ribbons wound around the multiple-armed candelabra standing either side of the iconostasis.

A service had been under way, but I had stayed only long enough to watch three priests come from the sanctuary. One of them had held the Gospels high for all to see, whilst the choir of six men chanted, one droning an impressive bass note.

The sun was well up by the time I returned to the hotel. As I arrived, a young boy of about eleven entered from the street to sing a kalanda. This was the real thing. He wore jeans and a loose shirt, and had a solemn and anxious expression. In his hand he held his triangle which he struck as he sang in a hoarse soprano -

> Today is Epiphany and inspiration
> and our Master's great joy.
> Down in Jordan river
> is the Holy Virgin
> with censers in her fingers
> and our Lord holding candles
> and praying to St. John
> "John, my Saint and Forerunner
> can you baptize a child of God?"
> "I can, I will and I bow
> and my Lord I pray
> to let me tomorrow rise up to Heaven
> to trample down the idols,
> to rain incense on the Heavens
> and come down to the river
> to baptize, You Christ."

Different kalanda are sung over Christmas, New Year and Epiphany. During this period there are believed to be mischievous sprites abroad known as kallikantzaroi. They are supposed to slip down chimneys and cause trouble during the twelve days of Christmas. To rid households of them the priest - or so they once did - visited each family armed with a cross and, using a sprig of basil, sprinkled holy water with it. In rural areas fields, vineyards, olive groves, cattle sheds and goat shacks were purified in this manner, in order to drive away these kallikantzaroi. Even if this holy water achieved little (or still achieves) it serves as a balm to the mind of worried peasant farmers.

It was ten o'clock when I went down to the Great Harbour for the Blessing of the Waters ceremony. Preparations were well under way. The road along the harbour was cordoned off, and the police were busy controlling the traffic and crowds. I took up a position close to where the procession would come from the cathedral, and pass on to a specially erected platform by the water's edge. A blue and white awning and several fluttering Greek flags marked the V.I.P.'s enclosure. Three frigates were positioned to surround the area into which the cross would be thrown. All the ships in port were a-flutter with flags and pennants (or 'dressed overall' to put it in nautical language).

Several contingents from the armed services marched past and took up their positions. The marching reflected many late nights of festivities. When commanded to halt they shuffled to a stop; and when ordered to turn to the left they more or less obeyed, except for one who turned to the right and had to about turn quickly. But in Greece nobody worries too much; they have the happy knack of remembering that it's all the same in a hundred years' time.

Dignitaries arrived, many of them in old cars driven by chauffeurs dressed casually. The British ambassador was embarrassingly smart in his shiny limousine flying the Union Jack. An interesting character approached the platform and stood for photographers; he carried a long twisted staff, and wore a cap and breeches and black leather boots; his chest was arrayed with medals, and I was told he was a V.I.P. from Crete.

An admiral arrived looking surprisingly dapper in his uniform, and wearing his sword of honour. A moment later I heard him being piped aboard, though to which ship I couldn't see for the crowds. Sailors lined the decks of each frigate.

From the cathedral the Liturgy for the Blessing of the Waters was being relayed so that all could take part in this religious occasion. I knew that in the cathedral were the Prime Minister and members of the government, together with local civic dignitaries and other V.I.P.s.

It was a lovely day and the sun shone and the sky was blue. Yes, it was chilly but, compared to England which had been under snow when I left, it was a summer's day. I was surprised there was no snow on any of the mountains around Athens, and was told it had so far been an exceptionally warm winter.

As I waited in the crowd, I began to wish that a priest would sprinkle holy water to subdue a tiresome unshaven fellow (a kallikantzaros?) standing beside me. He was insisting that I join him for coffee after the ceremony. I resorted to my usual practice under such circumstances of saying that I had a husband waiting for me back at my hotel.

It was a useful ploy. The day before I had had a similar problem when I'd been walking in a deserted area near Mikrolimani bay. There I had noticed an unshaven brute hanging around and I'd tried to hail a taxi. When one had at last stopped the thug had nimbly jumped into the back. It is customary in Greece for several people to share taxis.

"Where you from?" enquired the thug. When I'd told him I was from England he immediately spoke in very good English: "Ah! from England. You speak Greek very good!" Continuing in Greek I told him that in Greece the weather was very hot but in England it was freezing. This brought the response: "It is true that in England you are all cold - here in Greece we are very hot - you understand what I am saying?"

I suspected that I understood only too well. On that occasion too I had a husband waiting for me at the hotel which shut him up and he soon asked to be put down.

Eleven o'clock was nearing; at the stroke of eleven all the churches of the Orthodox world would throw the sacred cross into the waters, into rivers, reservoirs, ponds, lakes, the sea and, wherever appropriate, young men, shivering in their swimming trunks would dive in to retrieve it.

Short, spasmodic pealing of the cathedral bells prepared us for the big occasion. A line of government officials, town councillors and suchlike came down the road. Soon I could see banners approaching. A number of black-bearded priests in white robes and tall black headgear flanked the Archbishop who was a small figure in his glistening domed mitre, glimpsed every now and then below the level of the bushy beards of the priests.

As the Archbishop passed, people crossed themselves and the sailors presented arms to the cross, and a band struck up. The V.I.P.s passed out of sight as they mounted the platform. At the same time a marine band approached with a loud boom-boom of a drum. Beyond the crowds I could see a ferry-boat set sail for the islands. Those on board would be aware of the imminent Blessing of the Waters.

When the big moment came and the cross was thrown by the Archbishop into the Great Port of Piraeus, the cathedral bells and all the church bells of Greece pealed clashingly. At the same moment ships' sirens blasted, guns fired, the marine band played, and the drum bang-banged in a deafening cacophony of sound. So loud and so overwhelming was it, it seemed we were all drawn into the whirlpool of the moment by a sort of centrifugal force. A massive tingling sensation ran up and down my spine, and everybody crossed himself - thumb and first two fingers together, to the forehead, stomach, right breast, left breast and to the middle; women tended to put the palm of the hand to the heart as though sealing something within.

As sirens hooted and guns fired and bells clashed and bands played, a wide jet of water spurted out in a long arc from land to sea. In the clear blue sky I saw a single white dove flying, and much higher was the silver streak of an aeroplane: nature, human enterprise - all drawn into the moment of commemorating the Theophania (the appearance of God). Today the manifestation of Christ, Son of God Almighty, two thousand years ago the appearance of Apollo, son of Zeus, lord supreme.

When all was over I joined the throngs at the cathedral. At the top of the steps on either side of the entrance were two pale blue metal containers from which the faithful were drawing water. They filled every sort of vessel but mostly plastic bottles, in order to take this holy water home. They had complete faith in its purifying qualities and healing powers.

A massive queue had formed to get into the cathedral. I entered by a side door and saw that the queue was to see the large ornate silver cross, which was now laid on a red brocade-covered lectern on a raised dais. Joining the front of the queue I asked a nearby woman if I could take a photograph. She seemed to invite me to go up before her and, without more ado, but mumbling my apologies for jumping the queue, I got up on the dais and stood before the magnificent silver cross. I took two photos before performing the expected Orthodox ritual (the least I could do under the circumstances) and reverently kissed it and made the sign of the cross. Such acts, even from sceptics, are an acknowledgement that there is something greater than what is visible - a spiritual source to be tapped which is life enhancing.

I left the cathedral and returned to the quayside. The masses were now wandering onto the platform where the Archbishop had been with the V.I.P.s. It was a cheerful crowd, sauntering and enjoying the sunshine. Bright coloured helium-filled balloons were being sold; a Father Christmas wandered around; children were devouring candy floss, and street vendors were doing a brisk trade. I looked down into the murky waters where the cross had been thrown; the cross certainly had not visibly purified it.

I walked along the quay and watched the ships as they manoeuvred and set sail, or came in with their cargo. A newly arrived ferry-boat lowered its ramp to the quay and lorries and cars and foot passengers disembarked.

Life went on as usual in this busy maritime port. There was, though, a feeling of rejuvenation amongst the people, of faith and trust in a future blessed by the sign of the cross and the touch of the cross. Long before Christianity the cross had been a religious symbol of eternal life. That day had been a variation on a very old theme.

APOLLO OR ST. GEORGE

...AND THE PYTHON-DRAGON

CHAPTER

9

ARÁCHOVA

The priest's voice came down to us over the roof tops, relayed from the floodlit Church of Agios Georgios high up the village of Aráchova. We were there for the three day festival of St. George.

It was also Holy Week. At that precise moment, however, I was too busy haggling over the price of rooms to care what week it was. I had booked to stay with an 'agricultural' family in order to experience the festival from a local perspective but, due to an excess of family visitors, we'd been banished to an expensive self-catering apartment. The price per night was four times more than we'd budgeted for. As for the 'agricultural' side of the matter, I'd just been told by the son of the family that his father was, in fact, an electrician who owned two olive trees and a goat. I felt increasingly that we were being duped.

"It is too much?" enquired the son of the family politely. I was glad to see he looked shamefaced. "Then how much are you able to pay?" he asked pleasantly.

I was not used to haggling in English let alone in

Greek, and Harry had no idea what was being discussed. I had no wish to offend but threw out a figure considerably less than the one demanded. The son informed me we would find nothing cheaper in Aráchova, and left saying he would enquire of his mother and would return in the morning.

The priest's voice continued to invade the privacy of our apartment, wailing like a mosquito in and out of our consciousness, chanting its messages of sin and repentance, love and forgiveness; but his words seemed totally irrelevant as Harry sat down with pen and paper and worked out the rent if we stayed a week. The answer gave him palpitations.

"We could, I suppose, return to that pension at Delphi where we stayed before?" I suggested. Delphi was only a few kilometres away and there were frequent buses; it would be easy to return for the highlights of the three day festival of St. George.

Next morning we enquired at the pension. Had they a room? They had? How much? So little? We booked the room at once, collected our belongings and fled in a waiting taxi.

St. George's day that year coincided with Easter Sunday which meant that the three day festival would not get fully under way till the following day. We sat out on the terrace of our pension drinking coffee in the warm spring sunshine. The terrace overlooked a wide valley and dry river-bed filled with olive trees. From it we could see down to the port of Itea and the Gulf of Corinth, and back up to the wild terrain of the ancient Delphic oracle site and the Parnassos mountains.

Our landlady came out. "Christos anestei!" she said. "Aleithos anestei!" I replied. By now I was fluent when saying it. Her husband appeared with a watering-can and attended to his many terracotta pots of geraniums and roses. I again exchanged the Easter greetings and he presented me with the traditional red egg.

That morning families were seated along the roadside turning half-a-dozen spitted lambs (Paschal lambs) over their charcoal fires. Greek music blared from transistors, and wine flowed in happy communal camaraderie as they kept up the task of turning the carcases.

We made our way past these jolly revellers, and found a partly hidden goat track I'd been told about behind Delphi, which led to the lower slopes of Parnassos. Everywhere were wild flowers in profusion and the ground was a carpet of colours. The warmth of the spring sunshine seemed to accentuate the rugged distant mountains with their snow-capped peaks. All was a-buzz with the renewal of nature. The mating season had begun and insects flew around together in carefree copulation. Greece was bursting with regeneration.

We followed the track to a grassy plateau with fine views in all directions, with the ancient oracle site way below us. The sky was blue and there was a pleasant breeze.

We sat down on the grass and I told Harry a little about the extraordinary history of the Delphic oracle, the sacred precinct claimed by Apollo. Legend had it that it was there at Delphi that the monstrous Dragoness guarded the child born to Hera, wife of Lord Zeus. This child had been immaculately conceived when Hera, in one of her fits of jealous rage, this time because Zeus had given birth to Athena alone and without her involvement, had prayed to

Gaea (mother earth) that she too might have a child alone and without aid from Zeus.

In due course Hera's wish had been granted, and she'd immaculately conceived and given birth to Typhaon, a horrible creature, whom she'd entrusted to the Dragoness at Delphi. Somehow the two - Typhaon and Dragoness - became fused in people's minds and became Python. The first thing Apollo did when he came to Delphi was to slay the Dragoness-Typhaon-Python. Homer, in his Hymn to Apollo in which the monster was called the Dragoness, described her death: '...writhing in strong anguish, and mightily panting she lay, rolling about the land. Dread and dire was the din, as she writhed hither and thither through the wood, and gave up the ghost...'

The Christian version at Aráchova was that there had once been a monstrous dragon living in the locality (Delphi?) who had deprived the people of their water. All attempts to persuade him to spare enough for the locals had failed until he had set eyes on the king's daughter. If she was given to him, he would leave the water for the people, he'd said. The girl had been on the point of being sacrificed when St. George had miraculously arrived and slain the dragon.

It is interesting that the name George in Greek is Georgios and was an epithet of Zeus, Zeus Georgios, protector of the earth. The word is a compound of 'ge' or 'gaea' (earth) and 'ergein' (to work). So far as I know there was no such first name as George or Georgios before Byzantine times - in other words it was truly a 'Christian' name.

Down there in the ancient Delphic site, close by the temple of Apollo, was the Sacred Fountain at the centre of the sanctuary of Gaea, where it was said the dragon had stood guard over the water. The grandeur of the nearby towering Phaedriades rocks (twin crags from which water tumbled down a narrow gash into the Castalian spring) was a suitable lurking place for such a monster.

It was believed that Apollo, after slaying the Python-Dragon, took himself off to atone for the deed and served as a slave to Admetus, king of Pherae in Thessaly. There he stayed eight years and Admetus, recognizing in Apollo the qualities of a deity, treated him with the respect due to a god, with the result that Apollo saw to it that his flocks increased and his ewes dropped twin lambs - hence the belief that Apollo was protector of flocks. Today it is St. George who is protector of flocks (surprise!).

I pointed out to Harry that, in fact, there was little evidence that St. George had ever lived. He had supposedly been martyred in the third or fourth century, but it was not until the start of the Renaissance, that interest had reawakened in ancient Greek culture, and the legend of St. George slaying the dragon had become widespread - it was surely an echo from the story of Apollo?

I think my illuminating bits of information were going unheeded because, when I looked around, Harry was on his back with his sun-hat over his eyes and his mouth slacking open. The persistent, haunting sound of a hoopoe calling from the mountain came clearly and repeatedly on the air, and was infinitely more attractive than the rhythmic gurgle and whistle beside me. I lay back on the grass also and thought about the following day when we would be taking the bus to Aráchova to see the games, which were part of the celebrations in honour of St. George. In ancient times, of course, there'd been the Pythian Games in honour of Apollo.

We joined the crowds who were climbing up the slopes behind Aráchova. The village had come to life with bunting and clusters of brightly coloured helium-filled balloons tugging at their strings. Many villagers were in traditional costume. Some wore smocked or finely tucked grey tunics and on their legs, white woollen leggings with black tasselled garters at the knee, and clogs with large black pom-poms. Others wore black waistcoats over white full-sleeved fine lawn shirts and white pleated kilts (the fustanella), and also white woollen leggings and clogs.

From above we could look down on Aráchova which was an attractive huddle of russet coloured roof-tops, dominated by the dome of the Church of Agios Georgios. The village clung to the lower foothills of Mt. Parnassos, which then appeared to fall away to rise again as a range of hills beyond.

It was the old men's race (those aged over seventy) which drew the crowds. At the top of the slope officials held several black and white fat lambs to be presented to the winner of each race. These lambs were given by the local shepherds as a gift to the saint in gratitude for his protection of their flocks.

The gun fired and the old men set off. The race was not so much run as briskly walked. It was held on the site of an old battlefield, the starting point being the shrine where the bones of those who had fallen in the Greek War of Independence were kept.

A cheer went up and there was enthusiastic applause as the leaders out-paced those not strong enough to stay the course. The winner was a vigorous grey-head with clipped moustache, who climbed briskly with strong legs in their white woollen leggings and clogs. A close second was a colourful character in full dress costume. He had long straggly grey hair and a beard, and a smiling weather-beaten face. On his head he had a red cap fringed with gold tasselling set at a rakish angle. He wore a red brocade waistcoat over his white full-sleeved shirt, and the traditional white fustanella, leggings and clogs. He was fully armed with shot-gun, dagger and a belt of cartridges. He was, I was told, the appointed guardian of the icon of St. George.

I asked a young woman standing beside me about the previous day when the icon had been carried around the village by the people. I had read that the custom was to turn off the water serving the village, and that a song was sung in honour of the saint. At the words 'Dragon, set free the water that the revellers may drink', the water was turned on again to the village. The young woman knew nothing of this and asked her many relations standing nearby. Some said yes, whilst others shook their heads or looked puzzled.

We descended to the playing-field beside the church to watch the dancing of the old men. The winner of the race danced with his prize of a fat lamb slung comfortably around his shoulders. In the centre of the circle of dancers two great drums beat the rhythm, and two pipers blew instruments like small trumpets known as pipeizes.

"My uncle asks if you will join us for a drink?" said the young woman who by now had been joined by brothers and sisters, uncles, aunts and cousins. We went with them to the plateia. Harry and I got separated as more chairs were drawn into a large circle of relatives around two tables. Although Harry never spoke to foreigners if he could avoid it, it didn't stop children eager to speak English talking to him. He was put through the usual Greek inquisition of 'What's your name?' 'Where you from?' 'How old are you?' 'What work you do?'

I asked about the stories of St. George, and soon was into a lively discussion on the merits and power of Orthodox saints and miracles.

I was told how, during the last war, the inhabitants of the nearby village of Distomo had been massacred by the Germans. The German general, billeted at Aráchova, had intended to carry out a similar slaughter of the people of Aráchova but, during the night, St. George had come to him in a dream and had told him to spare the village. As a result not a soul had lost his life. After the war, the general had returned annually to the village for the saint's feast-day, until his own death a few years back.

They told me also about the battles fought in the Greek War of Independence which began in 1821. The military hero of the time had been a certain Georgios Karaiskakys - so his name-day would have been the feast-day of St. George. At any rate, thanks to the support and intervention of the saint, the Turks were repelled and the Greeks regained their freedom. I didn't point out that Lord Byron, revered by all Greeks for his support and help during this time, had also been George, but he'd caught a fever and died.

As we were into this religious discussion, I rather foolishly told them that there had been similar miracles in the past brought about by the old gods, and that at Delphi it was said that it had been the gods who'd caused thunder and lightning and had sent boulders tumbling from the pinnacles of the Phaedriades rocks, crushing the invading Persians and putting them to flight.

"I must tell my grandmother that!" said a bright-eyed comical sixteen year old youth beside me. "Since my grandfather he is dead she is in the church and it is the candles she lights and the saints she kisses. Now I say to her she must kiss the rocks at Delphi!" I was afraid I might be looked upon as a corrupter of young minds and changed the subject to Manchester United which brought me into favour with his uncle, followed by Posh and David Beckham which pleased his aunt.

I noticed Harry trying to understand the questions asked by two children; he could never quite tune his hearing in to English spoken by foreigners and had an expression of good-humoured non-comprehension. As by now his glass was empty, I thought it time to relieve him of flying the British flag of social pleasantries - time to return to Delphi. We agreed to meet on the last day of the three day festival, when the church would be giving a feast for the whole village, and the final celebrations would be performed in honour of the saint.

"How often do you drive up here?" I asked our taxi driver. He was a surly brute and from under his thick black walrus moustache came a grunt. I repeated the question, determined to have my 'Greek conversation' which would justify the price of the taxi. We were driving through the Parnassos mountains on the way up to the Korykaon cave high up its slopes.

Eventually there was a curt reply: "Two, three times each year." Greek men when they are not being charming and helpful can be quite impossible and ill-tempered.

The fare for the taxi was exorbitant but my

determination to see this cave which was said to be the original home of the Dragon, far outweighed the price of the taxi. He needed the money, I wanted to see the cave. To hell with money! So much? Harry was ready to object but saw fire snorting from my nostrils and backed down rapidly.

"We will pay you when you return for us," I told the surly brute and he gave me a surprisingly friendly nod of agreement. He pointed to a goat track and told us to climb up another twenty metres to find the cave. Then, with expert backing and turning of wheels he went bumping slowly away along the pot-holed road.

We were quite alone and stood like a couple of beetles on the mountainside with a view to a wide grassy plateau far below and snow-capped mountains beyond.

We climbed the steep track as instructed and saw the cave. It looked like a snarling mouth or monstrous throat. This then was the dwelling place of the old Dragon. I could envisage the creature living up there and defending the evils of the world. It was believed that this cave was one of many entrances to Hades.

The cave was also known as the Cave of Pan, the strange god who was half man, half goat, who roamed the mountains on cloven hooves and played the Pan pipes. 'Pan' is where the word 'panic' comes from.

For a while we wandered about the cave, a horrible vaulted cavity with dark hues of dampness staining the rock, an open jaw to the nether regions. It is believed that the worshippers of Dionysos had come up here for their strange rites, climbing the mountain tracks in their wild trance-like state for their orgiastic celebrations.

Through the cave entrance the sun shone; there outside was the 'Light of the world' and we were glad to get back to it. We sat against a boulder in the warm spring sunshine and I thought about the 'Light of the world' brought annually before the sanctuaries of Orthodox churches at the Resurrection service. That year at midnight the priest had appeared from the darkened sanctuary with his lighted candle, bringing the new 'Light' to the people, but the surge of those trying to get their candles lit from his had extinguished the priest's. Extinguished it! The 'Light of the world' had gone out! I had tried not to look on it as a bad omen, as an ominous death-knell. I mentioned these forebodings now. But Harry dismissed such nonsense, saying it was the natural consequence of too many people jostling forward.

"It must be boring seeing everything so clearly," I remarked.

"Thank the Lord one of us doesn't spin imaginary consequences into ordinary everyday happenings," he said.

"You just see the priest standing there with a lighted wick - how dull for you. There's no 'Light of the world' symbolism for you".

"No. Yes. Of course I can see what the idea behind it is."

"Well, I'm just suggesting that if there's symbolism in it being alight, then there's equally symbolism in it going out."

"You're just feeling argumentative," came the reply, and Harry tipped his sun-hat forward over his eyes to indicate the subject was closed.

I thought how Apollo had also brought light to the world. Phoebos Apollo as he was often called - Phoebos meaning 'bright' or 'pure'. It is strange that at Corinth where there was once a great temple of Apollo, there had also been an early Christian deaconess referred to by St. Paul as Phoebe (the feminine version of Phoebos). As far as I know there was no such first name until then; it is as though she was carrying forward in name a beacon of light from the pagan past, a name honoured by the inhabitants because it was identified with Apollo.

As we lazed, I heard singing somewhere on the lower slopes and not long after, a team of youths appeared up the goat track with torches and ropes. They told us they were about to explore a passage at the back of the cavern where there was an inner cave. It was very slippery, hence the rope.

I went with them into the gullet of the cave again, and was given a strong arm to pull me up to a ledge. I did not go further but watched the young men rope themselves together, and one by one the torches disappear into the gloom, down the gut, so to speak, to the inner stomach of this monstrous symbolic Dragon.

I slithered back down from the ledge, and was relieved to get out into the sunlight without being seized by evil forces, swooping me up like giant phantom hands to take me away down to Hades.

When the youths returned, matter of fact and triumphant at having done the trip to Hades and back, we learned they were boy-scouts and were camping further down the mountain. They had signed their names inside the interior cavern as was customary, and had returned with what I called the 'dragon's teeth', small stalactites. I was presented with one before they gathered up their ropes and left. We could hear them singing as they made their way down the steep slopes to their camp.

We began to walk back along the pot-holed track. It was flanked by firs and on one of the trees we saw mistletoe hanging. It was said that the goddess Demeter's daughter, Persephone, when returning from the subterranean kingdom of Hades, opened the gates of the underworld with the magic power of the mistletoe.

Grassy glades, carpeted with spring flowers, could be seen through the trees. There we found forget-me-not, asphodel, bird's eye, grape hyacinths, white and pink anemonies and iris. I sat amongst the flowers and picked a few as Persephone had done before Hades abducted her and dragged her screaming to his kingdom.

In due course we returned to the track and were met by our brute of a taxi driver. On this occasion, however, he had brought his wife and his mood was transformed. The surliness of the morning had vanished and all was jollity. We returned to Aráchova cheerfully discussing the merits of Scotch whisky which, he said, he drank every evening.

"You speak Greek very good," he said to me.

"I do?" I wasn't too sure I'd heard correctly.

"For how many years you learn Greek?"

When I told them six years they were full of praise.

"Only six years? Ah, she is so good!" cried the wife.

"Yes, she is very good! Bravo!" said my brute of a taxi driver.

I basked in the praise, and was now charmed by this man whose sullen features of the morning were miraculously transformed into smiles and friendliness.

It was the last day of the three day festival of St. George, and the day of the church feast. Harry was somewhere outside in the sun reading an old newspaper. He had, no doubt, found a corner out of the cold wind.

I was inside the Church of Agios Georgios, warming myself before the candles of supplication close to the icon of the saint set in a prominent position. The picture of St. George on a white charger slaying the dragon was the familiar one. The embossed silver frame was decorated with white and red flower-heads. Beside the icon was a silver reliquary said to contain the skull of the saint; it was either a very small skull, or it contained only pieces of skull.

"How is it decided to whom a church should be dedicated?" I once asked a Greek scholar doing her Ph.D. in London. She had been one of several lecturers at a study-day on Byzantine icons. She had looked slightly surprised by my question, then had answered confidently that it was dedicated to a saint whose relics the church possessed. "How can that be," I asked, "when there are so many churches dedicated to, say, Agios Georgios? How can they all possess a relic of the saint?" Some small relic would be sewn into the altar cloth, I was told. I wondered about the dedication of churches to symbolic virtues, such as the Parthenon to Agia Sophia. If there was no positive martyr or saint how could a church hold a relic? I put the question and was told that the bishop would give his permission and, as regards the Parthenon's early conversion and dedication to Agia Sophia (Holy Wisdom), it would have pacified the pagans to have had such a temple dedicated to the holy wisdom of God.

So what about the saints? Kuria Alezaki had said that to honour icons and petition saints should be a part of every-day life, as saints stood between mortals and the Almighty. But whenever I had a problem I went straight to the top: 'Oh, God! a pain! Oh, God! a problem!' To go to the top when one should start at the bottom, what a nerve!

My thoughts were interrupted by Harry tiptoeing towards me. His shoes squeaked which caused the women kissing or crossing themselves before the icon to pause in mid-act. Faces turned and Harry smiled and grimaced alternately as he tiptoed with exaggerated care towards me. He sat down with a crackling of his wind-proof anorak and whispered loudly in my ear that outside all was ready for the feast and I should come now if I wanted a seat. He also told me that he had eaten his own self-made sandwiches and wasn't going to risk germ-infested barbecued lamb. As the faithful turned from the icon they threw inquisitive glances at this stage-whisperer whose English was perfectly understood by many of them.

We left the warmth of the church and went out into the grip of the cold wind. From a terrace higher up, the smell of lambs being spitted over charcoal blew down on the wind. The bunting around the church and playing-field was fortunately well secured; the wind screamed through it as through the rigging of a sailing-ship.

Around the playing-field were trestle-tables and benches. All those wearing traditional costume were seated together at one table, whilst at another were priests and village dignitaries. Amongst those at the former was the guardian of the icon. As well as a dagger, shot-gun and belt of cartridges he now held a very long shepherd's crook. His brown weather-beaten face, grey locks of hair and long grey beard gave him an air of rascally dignity.

There was a great turn-out and those who could not find a seat stood. We were fortunate to be sitting, but it was difficult to anchor the paper plates and beakers. Picnic knives and forks flew through the air. Hunks of lamb were served and the beakers were filled with red wine. I enquired of my neighbour if he would like my slab of feta cheese as I had too much on my plate. It was lucky that I had lamb on my fork as my plate, with the rest of the contents, suddenly flew off on the wind amidst much laughter from those around me. Harry, who had been given a plateful despite trying to wave it away, went courageously through the motions of eating 'foreign germs' until he too managed to get his plate to fly away. This only brought hospitable villagers insisting he eat food from their plates, and a kindly woman offered him lamb off her fork which Harry in all politeness had to eat, all of which brought many smiles and nods of approval.

The priest rose in his black cassock and black kalimavki (Orthodox headgear). He had a plump, florid face and thick grey beard. He called for silence and the Resurrection hymn was sung. Then a poem, dedicated to St. George, was read. A little later there was another paean in honour of the saint, each verse sung with gusto, either by those at the priest's table or those in traditional costume seated with the guardian of the icon. At the end of each verse a gun was cheerfully fired in the air.

The comic sixteen year old youth we had met before sat opposite, and somehow the conversation came around to something that had been bothering me. Whilst sitting in church on the night of the Resurrection, I had had one leg crossed over the other. Soon a man had left the lectern where the choir stood, and had approached me and murmured, 'Parakalo', indicating I should uncross my legs. I had glanced sideways at the other women and had noticed that they all sat four square with their legs together.

"Tsst, tsst, tsst!" said my comic. "When you die you now go to hell!"

His sister on his other side leaned across. "Do not listen to him. But it is true it is a sin to cross the legs in the church."

"Why?" I asked.

She and her relations questioned each other, but no one knew why. I could only suppose it was an offence to the Cross or some such thing.

"Neither should you wave your hand with the palm facing towards anybody," said the girl.

"You must not wave as if you are a priest blessing the people," said my comic. "My grandmother would not like it."

"You must not listen to my brother. He is never serious!" his sister warned me.

When the feast was over the drums were beaten and the pipeizes played, and soon the village priest's black robed bulk moved out onto the playing-field, hands outstretched for others to follow, and the dancing began. The branches of trees bent to the wind; the Greek flag from its flag-staff rippled tautly in the teeth of the gale; the women in frilly, mantilla-like head-dresses, long white skirts and bright waistcoats, or red and gold embroidered pinafores, some wearing heavy gold coined necklaces, moved gracefully, their clothes billowing in the wind. We were invited to join in - a few steps sideways, leg across, then a small hop before moving onwards in a slowly rotating circle. Harry, although reluctant, was pulled out by my comic and his sister. After his first stumbling steps he soon got the rhythm and, with an optimistic smile, admitted happily that he preferred it to waltzing.

After a while the tempo of the dance increased and the young men of the village began to show off their skills. A handkerchief was held by one and gripped by another who displayed his strength by bending his body to the ground, his strong legs supporting him as his head went lower and lower. The handkerchief was strained to the limit as he passed under the raised arms of his companions. Another, the best looking in grey smocked jacket, white woollen leggings and clogs, and grey round cap set at an angle, bent backwards and then took off, one leg swinging high over the other. The girls kept up their own simple steps circling around and appeared not to notice this male spectacle. It seemed a sort of mating game when the male animal exhibits his strength, and the female pretends indifference but, nevertheless, perceives out of the corner of an eye.

I was introduced to an American who had written a history of the village. He told me that it was believed that the Church of Agios Georgios was built on the site of an old temple of Apollo, and that a column from the temple still stood in the church. He took us inside and pointed it out, which only added to my St. George and Apollo connection.

A peal of bells from the church and we went out to find the musicians leading the people from the playing-field. The priest followed and, with hands held, the villagers circled the church three times singing the patronal festival song; every now and then a shepherd raised his gun in the air and fired a shot.

After the third tour of the church, the priest and musicians led the procession down the many steps from terrace to terrace to the lower road. Traffic was stopped as the cheerful villagers followed the priest who was now flanked by shepherds. It would end, I was told, at the plateia where there would be more dancing.

By now I felt blotto from concentrated information, red wine and the persistent cold wind, and was ready to leave. We said good-bye to the Comic and his family and exchanged addresses for future English-Greek correspondence. Before the priest, shepherds and villagers filled the road and prevented our return to Delphi, we quickly found a taxi and left. I fell back on the seat and closed my eyes, only to open them to find Harry peering closely at me.

"Are you all right?" he asked.

"It's only the wine, you fool!"

"Oh, is that all it is? Well, that's something we can thank St. George for!"

"Ayios Yeoryios," I murmured.

"Ayios Yeoryios? Milate Ellenika?" barked the taxi driver, looking at me in the driving mirror.

"Prospatho mono,"(I try only) I replied. I pulled myself together and leaned forward to take this last opportunity for a taxi fare's worth of Greek conversation.

But from then on the taxi driver's staccato bursts of questions hit the usual blank wall in my head, and I was glad when we were put down at Delphi. It was Churchill who said that spoken Greek sounded like a pile of crashing plates. The rest of the afternoon was spent flat on my back sleeping off the festivities of St. George.

That evening we met up with a bunch of English ramblers, whose leader was a retired Admiral. We learned that they were returning to Athens the following day, in time for a late afternoon flight. An we too were flying home that day, though several hours later, the Admiral suggested we travel with them on their coach. The word 'money' wasn't mentioned, but I knew Harry was thinking it would be a saving and worth the extra few hours at the airport.

I believed I could take advantage of this new arrangement to see the Monastery of Daphni, once a temple of Apollo (Daphneos Apollo). I asked the Admiral if it was possible to stop off at this famous monastery a few miles out of Athens. The Admiral exuded confidence and authority. Nothing could be easier, how interesting, it would be his pleasure to ask the driver, he said, and he rubbed his hands together in anticipation, eager to see what he could do.

I thought I was doing everyone a favour by giving them this opportunity to see this Monastery of Daphni. In due course we came to the spread-eagled suburbs, and the industrial area of Athens. I saw a sign-post to Eleusis, and glimpsed the small acropolis below which had once been the sanctuary of Demeter, goddess of corn. If not actually driving along the Sacred Way, on which the faithful of old would have come in procession from Athens for the Greater Mysteries of Demeter, we were at any rate driving alongside it, and sometimes on it.

When we arrived at the monastery, the Admiral came down between the seats and told us this was where we got off. It was unexpected, as we'd thought we were all to get out. A quick re-think. Harry would remain with the luggage, whilst I did the monastery, as I was the one wanting to see it. I need not stay long, and would then get a bus and meet up with them at the Acropolis, which was the Admiral's plan for his ramblers.

"Give me what money you have," I said to Harry, and seized his last few thousand drachma as they emerged from his wallet. I had five hundred on me, which was not enough should I need a taxi. I leapt out, and waved back at the smiling English faces as the coach pulled away.

I left the noisy traffic whipping along the road into

Athens, and approached the monastery set back amongst olive trees and cypresses. An aura of peace pervaded the place as I entered the courtyard with its surrounding cloisters. I saw no monks, and found the church undergoing repairs to its famous mosaics; the building was stripped of all its furnishings. I was glad the others hadn't stopped off too.

Despite the work going on, the interior was impressive. The whole building was dominated by the vast central dome, with the mosaic portrayal of Christ Pantokrator (Christ the all powerful) staring down watchfully, one hand raised in blessing, the other holding a richly decorated Gospels. There were mosaics of biblical scenes on every wall surface, including the one of Christ rising from Hades where he had descended for three days after his crucifixion. Under Christ's feet was the recumbent figure of the old god Hades, whilst Adam and Eve were being drawn up by the hand. Symbolically Christ was releasing the world from sin and death, though why it was necessary to be delivered from sin and death still baffled me. My only thought was that the human mind was incapsulated in a seed-pod of Hope, and that was what the scene represented, man's profound Hope.

In the old Greek story, all the sins and diseases of the world were originally stored in Pandora's box. When it was opened, these all flew out, but Hope remained inside. In Greek mythology, Pandora was the first woman and, like Eve in the Old Testament, was destined to create problems by introducing sin into the world. Why was it always a woman who was blamed?

I wandered out and around the monastery. An old fluted Ionic column was pointed out to me as being original to the ancient temple of Daphneos Apollo - Apollo, who gave guidance to men through his oracles, and who also brought Hope to mankind.

I looked at my watch. It was time to catch the bus into Athens if I was to meet up with Harry and the Admiral's group at the Acropolis. I couldn't resist buying a book about the Daphni monastery, and now had even less drachma left. But I had Hope.

I waited with a young family for the bus and, when finally it came, we boarded it together. The eleven year old son of the family sat beside me. Soon I had asked him if he knew where I should get off for the Acropolis and, as with all Greek children, he was eager to speak English. I asked him his name. "Apollo," he answered. "Apollo? Really Apollo?" I asked. "Really Apollo," he replied, and told me how his father was a great enthusiast about ancient history and the gods. His mother, who was seated with a friend, smiled at us from a far seat.

This young Apollo was a great guide. To get to the Acropolis, he told me, I must do this and that, turn left and right. It had been the custom of the old god to give his oracular advice in riddles, and it was up to the individual to interpret the words as best he could.

I got off the bus and waved to Apollo as he continued his journey. I began to walk. I couldn't for the life of me remember Apollo's instructions. I first found myself in a market, which I supposed was Monastiraki. There were cages of exotic birds, leather goods, meat stalls, fish, fruit, clothes - . It was very hot and I thought it vital to invest in a bottle of water as it appeared I had a long walk. I now had only four hundred drachma. Still I had Hope.

I hurried on, sucking the cold water through a straw, to refresh myself. When I reached the Acropolis, there was no sign of Harry, the Admiral or the coach. I walked on to Syntagma Square soothing my nerves and hunger with the water which was now getting low. The bus for the airport* finally arrived and, about twenty minutes later, I was put down and hurried into the building to find Harry. No Harry. I enquired of an official and showed him my flight ticket. Oh, you should be at the other airport, I was told. The other? What other? I should get another bus; the airport was only about ten minutes away, he said. I felt cross that I had paid for a bus ticket, having expressly asked the driver for the international airport and he'd put me down at the wrong place. But I had Hope.

I caught the next bus, paid for another ticket, and was whisked off further and further, until I finally arrived at the airport which I thought looked familiar. I got out and hurried through all the entrances, but still no Harry. I showed my ticket to the nearest sympathetic looking traveller who said at once that I should not be at that airport but at the other. The other? How dare they fool about with me like this! Quick! on to the bus returning to the first airport. I looked at my watch. By now it was about three-fifty. Check-in time was four-fifteen. Then I remembered that my watch was unreliable as the battery had been running down. I asked somebody the time. What? Ten past four?

"Are you going to England - to Heathrow?" I asked a smiling Chinaman beside me. "Noy, I meet flend. Where you go?" "I am flying Olympic Airways to Heathrow," I said. "I meet flend on island of Palos," said the smiling face. "Well, I am going to Heathrow - I hope," I repeated. "Ah, Heathlow - you hope." And the smiling slit-eyes turned to gaze out of the window.

As we approached the airport, I was reassured by the many Olympic circles displayed over the building. I hurried in, rushing to its various check-ins, departure

* It was before the modern airport was built for the Olympic Games 2004

points - but no Harry. Finally, brandishing my ticket before a young uniformed woman behind a desk - by now the Greek language had quite forsaken me - I told her I wanted to get to England. She examined my flight ticket and said, "You are at the wrong airport. You should go to - ." Seeing my agitation she said soothingly, "There is no problem. Outside you take the bus. Or you may take a taxi."

I asked her to write down in Greek exactly where it was I should go. I sucked up the last drops of water from the bottle and dropped it into a litter-bin.

Outside in the heat again I hailed taxis, but each pointed to the queue waiting for them. I hadn't the money for one anyway, but thought I could worry about that later. I told a couple of idle men that I wanted a taxi and quick! They said I should go to the head of the queue; but advised me not to waste money on a taxi when there was a bus which would soon be leaving. There is no problem, they said, amused by my anxieties, all will come right. It was all very well for them, they had saints to call on. I had - "God Almighty! get me to this blessed airport!" The words were automatic. Subconsciously God was always there, however much I tussled with the reality of him.

I was still (without any doubt in my mind) armed with Hope as I hurried onto the bus, showed the driver the written words where I wanted to be taken, bought another ticket with the last of my money, and sat down and waited. A newly arrived plane from somewhere meant a crowd of bemused travellers were queuing to get on the bus. Each traveller had to buy a ticket; each had problems with the currency, or with change. Half an hour later we were off. By now I was recognizing the landmarks - Glivadha - Golf course - Airport -

At last the bus drew up beside this now familiar airport flying a line of international flags, with one military tank parked outside to show Greek power. I leapt off the bus and rushed to wherever one rushes to find waiting passengers.

I saw Harry at last. He was absorbed in an English newspaper; it was his way of coping with stress. I fell on his neck, destroying the paper.

It seemed to me then that the whole of life - yes, the whole of it - consists of making plans and trying to fulfil them. If there is God, or if there is no God, all rests on Hope which, if clobbered, creates another head of Hope like the Hydra. Even death cannot be seen as final, so long as the living mind, with Hope at its head, is there to conquer it.

KATAKLYSMA FESTIVAL

CHAPTER

10

CYPRUS

I wanted to arrive at Paphos like Aphrodite from the sea but time, finances and Harry prevented it and we descended instead from the sky. We were met at two-thirty in the morning by a stalwart friend who drove us to her flat in Larnaka. As an ex-patriot she'd lived in Cyprus ten years, but hadn't explored it so wanted to join us on our trip around the Greek part of the island.

Despite being suddenly widowed a few years back; despite a pending court case regarding property; despite several abdominal operations, she soldiered on alone with remarkable fortitude and energy and said she was an atheist. She never for a moment regarded her misfortunes as a judgement from on high, but as part of life.

I liked her unruffled sense of humour, and admired her stoicism. I use the word 'stoicism' deliberately because it was there in Larnaka that Zeno, founder of the Stoic philosophy, was born 335 B.C.

The Stoics never demanded a stiff upper lip as is supposed by the word 'stoic' today, but believed that nature was controlled by divine reason and that humans had a spark of the divine within them. Man's duty was to lead a virtuous life in harmony with this to achieve happiness.

"So what are your plans for this trip?" asked the Stoic the next day.

"Food and rest," said Harry hopefully.

I showed her an itinerary that I'd made after considerable ponderings over books of information and maps at home. As we were at Larnaka, an area called Idalion some twenty kilometres away, was top of the list.

"What happens at Idalion? I've never heard of the place," the Stoic remarked.

"It's where Adonis, the lover of Aphrodite, was killed by a wild boar," I said. "It's marked by a sanctuary."

"Well, you know best. I'm just the chauffeur, you tell me where to go."

The hills around the main Larnaka-Nicosia road were chalk-coloured and barren, with no trace of the forests in which Adonis was said to have hunted wild boar. The Stoic pointed to a distant hill and a chapel from which a Turkish flag flew.

"That's the Turks cocking a snook at the Greeks," she said. "There's no greater insult the Moslems can inflict, than to fly their flag from some Christian chapel."

For a visitor to Greek-held Cyprus there was no sign of the struggles that occurred in 1974 when the Turks invaded the island. The only problem a traveller is faced with today is that, if he wants to cross the border, then he can only do so after a great deal of form-filling, and on the understanding that he returns by five p.m. the same day.

The car windows were open and, although only mid-May, the hot arid air fanned our faces without cooling us. We turned off the main road and headed for the barren hills and the Turkish border. The Stoic was driving, whilst I tried to act the part of navigator. We saw no sign to direct us to the sanctuary site which I knew existed. Eventually, having gone back on our tracks several times, we found ourselves grinding uphill along a badly pot-holed narrowing track, and I said I'd get out and walk.

"Your wife, I can see, is determined to go where the car cannot," said the Stoic with calm patience. Then she added, "You'd better take this water if you don't want to expire in this treeless wasteland."

A warm dusty breeze marginally cooled me, and I was glad of the exercise. There was a fantastic view out over the plain where traffic whizzed along the main Larnaka-Nicosia highway. I walked on up, heading towards a couple of columns which seemed the most likely remains of a pagan sanctuary. In my mind I visualized the tragedy, the beautiful youth and the grief-stricken goddess beside his dying body. Tragedies, which are far removed from ones own reality, are fascinating.

There were several legends concerning Aphrodite's amorous adventures, but none better known than her love for Adonis. Persephone (Demeter's daughter) also loved Adonis, and was bitterly jealous when she learned that he preferred Aphrodite. When, therefore, Adonis went hunting one day in the forests in these parts, Persephone, in a green-eyed monstrous fit, turned a wild boar on him with fatal consequences. On hearing the news, Aphrodite ran to where Adonis lay dying and, in an outpouring of grief, wherever her tears fell it is said white lilies grew (some say white roses), and from the blood of Adonis came red anemones.

I reached the area where I'd seen the columns, only to find they were not part of an ancient sanctuary site but the construction of a pseudo-portico for an up and coming luxury hotel. Reluctantly, I had to admit defeat in my search, and leave the site of Adonis' death to the imagination. The imagination was certainly more fertile than the reality of these stony barren hills.

The Stoic was a great companion and trod the tightrope in a fine balancing act between keeping the peace with Harry's unwillingness to advance into the unknown, and encouraging my enthusiasms. "We must humour her," she would say to Harry. "Your wife has a plan and she must be allowed to follow through with it."

Two days later we were at Paphos. Early the first morning I set out alone to commune beside the Rock of Aphrodite where, it is claimed, Aphrodite rose from the waves. It wasn't until I'd sat like Rodin's 'Thinker' for some fifteen minutes, that I noticed another rock further away and realized I 'was in error', as a German tourist kindly informed me.

The coastal road passed the spot and a large hoarding visible to every passing motorist with his wits about him (or her), informed drivers of the location where the goddess of love had emerged from the waves. Frankly, it mattered little which rock. It wasn't as if Aphrodite was going to rise again and I needed to be ready for her.

I was really more interested in how stories fed the imagination, and how the imagination could take off with poetic fancy.

When Aphrodite rose from the waves, it is said that she was welcomed ashore by the Horae (daughters of Zeus) who 'clad her about in immortal raiment, and on her deathless head set a well-wrought crown...and when they had thus adorned her in all goodliness they led her to the Immortals, who gave her greeting when they beheld her, and welcomed her with their hands...' (Homer's Hymn to Aphrodite). There's nothing more poetic than that to feed the imagination!

Aphrodite may be thought Greek but, in fact, she originated in the Near East where she was known as Astarte. She first went to Greece to the island of Kythera, and from there on to Cyprus. In the mountains of Lebanon it was said that the River Adonis ran red every spring with the blood of Adonis (in reality it was from red soil washed down by flood waters at the time of year when the hills were carpeted with red anemones). But it was believed that Adonis wasn't really dead. An annual festival celebrated his death and resurrection. There was first a day of mourning - much as today people mourn the crucified Christ on Good Friday - then the day of joy at his Resurrection.

So I sat musing as I stared out to sea at the correct Aphrodite Rock. The sun was by now well up and cast its brilliant and sparkling path towards me along the calm and tideless sea. A white dove (emblem of Aphrodite) flew swiftly overhead against the blue sky. What, I wondered, would life be like without imagination? A dull progression from day to day with nothing more?

"Your wife wants to see the Church of Agia Paraskevi, so we must find it," said the Stoic later on that morning. "If we don't she'll never forgive us."

"We're looking for the village of Ierokypos which is

just outside Paphos," I said

"We'll have to turn back."

"My wife doesn't have to see every church."

"I don't want to see every church. But I do have to see this one. Would you like me to leave you here by the sea and hunt it out on my own?" I suggested, in an attempt to sound reasonable.

"No, we'd better stick together," said Harry. "We'll only lose you otherwise."

"Such is the perversity of the male. He doesn't want, but doesn't like to be without," murmured the Stoic.

The church was eventually discovered hidden in the suburbs of Paphos. Ierokypos (meaning 'holy garden') was no longer a village but a congested extension of the city. Here had been Aphrodite's holy gardens filled with flowers and trees and tended by young girls. Pilgrims, arriving at the port of Paphos, would have followed the ancient pilgrim's way to her great sanctuary and temple, a few kilometres further east which we ourselves were about to do.

Here there had also been a cave and Holy Spring (now sealed off thanks to a modern sewage system) where pilgrims would have offered sacrifice before continuing on to her major temple. These holy waters were believed to be blessed in Christian times by St. Paraskevi, and had cured diseases of the eyes. Perhaps it is coincidence that Aphrodite's feast-day had been Friday (or so I've read) and the Church of Agia Paraskevi (a female saint) means Friday and also 'holy preparation'.

The Church of Agia Paraskevi was an astonishing five-domed building from the ninth century, with walls four feet thick. In the central dome was painted the new 'queen of the heavens' (the Virgin Mary) with the infant Jesus.

Even Harry and the Stoic were impressed by this five-domed, grey stone building with its impressive ancient frescoes and icons. It breathed antiquity and holiness, and imbued a sense of spirituality in the hardest hearts. The Stoic said: "She's right, you know, it's a gem." And Harry said: "Hum, not bad," in a typically English understatement.

We drove on to the famous sanctuary and temple of Aphrodite, which was set on a rise of land well back from the sea. Compared to the Church of Agia Paraskevi in its busy suburban setting, here all was in ruins. It was difficult to know what to focus on or, when focused, whether it was worth the attention. Adjoining the sanctuary was a tiny grey-domed church. Now called the Katholiki it had once been dedicated to Panagia Aphroditissa (the All Holy Aphrodite).

I told Harry and the Stoic about the goings-on that had occurred at Aphrodite's annual festival. Before marriage it had been the custom for young virgins to adorn themselves most beautifully and come to the temple and sit demurely, whilst men filed past them. When a male eye fancied a particular girl he had only to throw a coin into her lap, whereupon the girl would give him her hand, and she'd be led away to a booth where she lost her virginity. A blind date if ever there was one, and there was no question of refusing the man.

"Good God!" said the Stoic, "how gross!"

"It was the custom and, therefore, wasn't frowned on," I explained. "It was a way of initiating young girls into the sanctity of love and sex. In fact, it was regarded as a goddess-given privilege and honour, and was performed by all classes, the wealthiest and the poorest alike. They were forbidden to marry until this initiation had been completed under the watchful eye of the goddess of love."

We wandered despondently amongst the ruins for a while. Nothing was easily identifiable. Eventually, I asked the girl who was selling postcards, if she could tell me where to find an ancient stone to which, until comparatively recently, nursing mothers having difficulties with breast feeding, had come to light candles and pray to the 'Virgin who gives Milk'. I was interested because in antiquity the local women used to petition Aphrodite at her cult stone (a large conical stone now removed to a museum), addressing her as Panagia Galaktariotissa (the All Holy Lady who gives Milk). The girl selling postcards wasn't going to leave her post and pointed through a window to some block of stone - which of the many, I couldn't really tell - and dismissed my enquiry as one not worth wasting time on. I began not to care anyway.

"She's tiring. It won't be long before you can have a snooze," said the Stoic to Harry.

I had to admit that the poetic imagery of Aphrodite, goddess of love - the beauty of the Venus of Milo in the Louvre, and other inspired sculptures of Aphrodite - far outshone the reality of her now defunct and ruined sanctuary.

"Ah, the woman's making for the car, and Harry's got that gleam in his eye when he knows food is next on the agenda. The things we feel obliged to do in the name of love!" sighed the Stoic.

The Stoic knew of a hotel in the hills north-west of Paphos within easy reach of the coast and the Troodos mountains. It was on the outskirts of the village of Droushia. Harry's eyes lit up as soon as we arrived. The great attraction was a swimming-pool surrounded by sun-beds and a bar. It had British army, tourists, affluence and hygiene written all over it, and Harry flung himself with zest into the pool, swam two lengths and came out and ordered a drink from one of several hovering waiters.

"I thought Harry would like this place," said the Stoic, whose eyes were hidden by sun-glasses and whose figure left a great deal to be desired in a bathing-suit. "One vodka, please," she said to the waiter.

I was happy that everybody else was happy, but tried to keep my mind on the things I'd planned to do whilst in Cyprus. There were several monasteries to be seen, and the Akamas peninsula to be walked, a favourite spot of Aphrodite's.

The village of Droushia was originally inhabited by Arcadians from the Peloponnese. After the Trojan War they had apparently sailed disastrously off course and ended up on Cyprus - the opposite predicament to the Virgin Mary, who had been invited by Lazarus to Cyprus, but who had ended up on Mt. Athos (the Holy Mountain). The Arcadians had been a pastoral people and so had come up to these hills.

The Trojan War itself was, of course, the consequence of lust. When Aphrodite promised the most beautiful mortal woman in the world to Paris (son of the King of Troy), so long as he chose her as the fairest of the goddesses in a contest between herself, Athena and Hera, he fell for it - the others had promised him such mundane things as power, victory and wisdom. The most beautiful woman was Helen (wife of Menelaus, king of Sparta, King Agamemnon's brother). When Helen and Paris ran off together, the Greeks demanded satisfaction, and the result was the Trojan War. The war lasted ten years during which the gods and goddesses of Olympus took sides and Aphrodite was wounded. She had been trying to shield her beloved mortal son from certain death at the hands of the mighty Diomedes. Her son was the consequence of an amorous adventure with a shepherd on Mt. Ida near Troy.

"I suspect we're not going to be allowed to idle for long," remarked the Stoic. It was evening, and we were sitting out on the hotel terrace. "So what plans do you have for us?" she asked lazily.

"To walk in the Akamas peninsula."

"Is it a suggestion or an order?"

"Nobody has to come with me, but I must explore the region. It's where Aphrodite used to bathe in her secret Grotto. They say Adonis first set eyes on her there when she was bathing nude."

"Another vodka for me," said the Stoic. "I must fortify myself against tomorrow's gruelling demands."

Night was coming on and, from our terrace, I gazed out at the darkening outline of the Akamas peninsula. The lights of a fishing village spread-eagled along the coast were becoming brighter in the twilight. A moon hung in the sky above Akamas, together with the Evening Star. The night was balmy, and this lounging business with drinks was going to my head. I was feeling unusually idle. I was aware that the Stoic and Harry were colluding together to undermine my itinerary.

"Another vodka for you too?" asked the Stoic.

"A tomato juice," I replied. "But I don't need anything. I'll wait until supper."

"Dinner, dear. Here they serve dinner haute-cuisine, not supper. God! this is a dream-world up here looking out over the landscape with the moon and, I suppose, that must be Venus? Love is in the air! I hope I'm not intruding being here with you? But I wouldn't miss it for the world." We assured her that we were at the contented stage of matrimony, and didn't need to be alone - in fact spent most of our time alone together and enjoyed outside company.

"Romeo, Romeo, wherefore art thou, Romeo?" murmured the Stoic, searching the faces of the men around, and resting her gaze on a solitary male figure hidden behind a newspaper. But the newspaper was shaken and the pages rearranged, and she saw an elderly, bald-headed lean and bespectacled face of a man in a sports vest.

"No, he will not do at all. The moon! the Evening Star! but no romance. Oh, dear!"

We had dinner and continued to be cosseted and waited on deferentially. In the middle of the meal the table went one way and then the other, and I glanced at Harry who was looking at the ceiling where the overhead lights swung gently.

"Just an earth tremor," said the Stoic, continuing with her food. "We're always having them in Cyprus. Not to worry!"

It was eerie. How did we know it wouldn't develop into a full-blown earthquake? "You don't," said the Stoic, "but I wouldn't lose any sleep over it, if I were you."

We didn't - well, not much. It made me aware of our mortality and the great divide between life and death, fitness and mutilation. In the event of an earthquake the high ceiling of our bedroom would come crashing down, and I didn't relish the idea of disappearing into a pile of rubble. A small prayer of appreciation for being spared (so far) was in order. 'Thank you, thank you', was no bad thing on occasions, and this was one of them.

The following morning we set out early in the direction of Akamas, driving down from the hills to Latchi by the sea. From Latchi we followed the coast road to the start of the Aphrodite trail. A few metres along the trail we found ourselves already at the Grotto. It was disappointing to find it so accessible; I had imagined having to walk far into the peninsula before coming across it.

Already over hot despite the short walk, we sat down beside the water and stared at the clear aquamarine pool, and leaned down to cool our hands in the cold spring. Water trickled and dripped down the surrounding rocks. Bamboos grew around the spot, and a fig tree hung its boughs over it. There was nothing but the sound of water and doves cooing. It was a place for deep-felt emotions and amorous advances, but Harry was not the man for the moment. As we were the only ones there I took off my sandals and dipped my feet into the cold water, defying a notice forbidding it, to which Harry said he thought by the look of my feet I could do with a spell at the chiropodist. Chiropodist? I looked at me feet with renewed interest and realized that they were not exactly those of a nymph. But they got me around. "Very serviceable," I declared defensively.

Where was this thing called 'love'? Years of marriage hadn't exactly done much for romance. But love has many facets like a diamond, and to expect the love of youth to persist is the first obstacle to be overcome by the average married couple. Love changes, just as humans do as they battle their way through life; through careers, babies, teenage offspring and retirement; through the tough times and the moments of plain sailing; through the happy times of what presents to give for Christmas, to the boring grumbles about extravagance.

A young couple arrived with their arms about each other. I put my sandals on again and watched the couple as they stared down into the waters of Aphrodite's Grotto. How long would they stay together, I wondered? Would they marry or drift apart and find other partners? This love thing was extraordinarily powerful when it was new and untried.

"If we're to do the trail, you two had better stop daydreaming. Come on now!" called the Stoic who was sitting inelegantly with her skirts around her thighs. "Somebody give me a hand up."

Harry and I both obliged and soon we began the trudge up a rocky path amongst stunted pines. Certain plants or trees were identified with labels and, every now and then, we came to vantage points where we could look across to the sea, to inlets and small coves where the water was like green shot-silk, or shades of sapphire and turquoise.

The trail took us higher and higher and then, after an hour, began to descend, until we came finally to a magnificent glade with a huge old oak tree and a spring. This was Pyrgos tis Rigaenas (the Shelter of the Queen). It was here, so it is said, that Aphrodite rested after she had bathed in her Grotto. It was shadowy and cool under the branches of the great oak, an oasis of charm after the clamber along the scorched rocky track. All around were tall pine trees with a gentle breeze soughing through their slender branches. Tiny black birds, with yellow breasts and red spots on their cheeks, flitted about from branch to branch. Close by there were the ruins of an old medieval monastery.

A young Dutch couple arrived. They intended to walk on up to the crest of another rocky peak, and from there to return along the coastal path. I knew it would be foolhardy to try the longer trek home in the midday sun, but couldn't resist going with them to see the view from the top.

"Be it on your own head," said the Stoic ominously, whose round face was puce and her hair damp under her sun-hat. Harry was seated on the ground and wasn't going anywhere, so I set out alone with the Dutch couple.

Thinking myself strong, and showing off that age could manage what the young could do, I strode up the track keeping an eye out for snakes and, in order to achieve my goal, kept up the pace higher and higher until wham! A sudden whirling of the senses, and the rocks seemed to spin around. I was suddenly faced with the fact that I was mortal. To be unable to continue was a new experience.

I managed to stagger to the shelter of a sparse fir, drank from my bottle and wanted to be sick. When the Dutch couple looked back I waved feebly, and indicated I was turning back. They called 'good-bye!' and strode on up.

Harry hadn't been happy about this trek into the heat where the sun's rays bounced back off the rocks, and had been watching my progress and now lack of it. When he saw I was stretched out flat he came to the rescue. This was love!

I was on the border line of the great divide, and gathering the gods to me. "Oh, God, I've been a bloody fool! Oh, God! I still have to write about Aphrodite! Oh, Aphrodite, I want to write about God!"

"My own silly fault," I said, as Harry heaved me up and more or less carried me back to the cool shelter of the glade. I lay out on the ground under the shadow of the trees, whilst the others discussed my predicament as though I wasn't there.

"She's obviously dehydrated," said the Stoic. "It can be fatal if not treated. I imagine she hasn't done this before?"

"She saw the doctor because she had dizzy spells last year," Harry said. "He didn't seem to panic."

"They're not paid to panic over their patients. But if you ask me, the old girl's just overdone it. If she's not better soon we'll have to get help."

"I will be better," I said. I was beginning to feel hungry, and asked for a marmite sandwich and a banana. This was brought to me promptly, and I realized there were some benefits in being ill.

"Your wife is on the mend," said the Stoic. "If we wait till later, I think she'll manage the walk back."

"Don't fuss. I'm fine really," I said

"No, we won't fuss," said the Stoic. "Here, drink some more water," and she put a hand under my head and helped me to sit up. "And eat these salted peanuts," she said. "We're not fussing, we just want to err on the side of prudence." And she wet a cloth from the spring and plonked it on my forehead, and told me not to argue but to do as I was told for once.

Several hours later, with the Stoic fanning my face and Harry holding my arm, we ventured out into the late afternoon sun. "We're not fussing!" repeated the Stoic, "only trying to make sure you make it to the road. We've two or three kilometres. How are you feeling?"

"I'm all right for the moment," I said, totally unsure of myself.

There were narrow tracks where the rocks fell away steeply which I manoeuvred on all fours. Then Harry took my arm and the Stoic fanned my face, and we carried on together, putting on an act of jolly camaraderie by smiling as other hikers passed us. Every twenty or thirty paces the Stoic called a halt and I was ordered to rest.

By the time we reached Aphrodite's Grotto, I was feeling almost normal.

"Almost normal, she says!" said the Stoic. "That's bad news for us."

We got into the car.

"Sure you're feeling better?" asked Harry. I nodded.

"Don't ask the woman!" admonished the Stoic. "Tell her she is close to death, it's the only way!"

The following day I felt fit and well, but knew I was being closely watched by the other two. In order to throw off this shroud of concern, I threw politics into the conversation at breakfast. Wouldn't they like to see the village of Panagia, where Archbishop Makarios had been born? Harry, I knew, would enjoy a foray into the political and historical past of Cyprus, which the British had held for no better reason than they hadn't wanted any other country to have it. Archbishop Makarios had rallied the Greek Cypriots in favour of Enosis (unity with mainland Greece) then later, had encouraged Colonel Grivas with his EOKA campaign against the British forces.

My suggestion was designed to get them up to the fringes of the Troodos mountains because, near to Makarios' village, was the Monastery of Panagia Khrysorroyiatissa.

"Remember your health!" warned the Stoic.

"I haven't forgotten it. I'm not about to climb a mountain, I'm merely looking at a monas- at museums," I corrected.

Harry fell for the bait and, leaving the Stoic having a day of rest by the swimming-pool, we drove up to Panagia. I spent the first part of the morning with Harry examining photographs and bits and pieces of Makarios' life then, at a moment when Harry was totally engrossed, I told him of the nearby monastery which I would just take a quick look at. He hardly noticed I was gone.

The monastery was founded in the twelfth century by a monk called Ignatius. He'd originally lived as a hermit on a mountain, but on the night of the Virgin Mary's feast-day, 15th August, 1152, he saw a light on the shores near Paphos. A light from heaven guided him to a small natural harbour near to Aphrodite's sacred garden, Ierokypos, where he discovered a miraculous icon of the Virgin Mary which had come in on the waves from Asia Minor to escape the Iconoclasts (hater and destroyer of icons). Like Aphrodite who'd risen from the sea, so now the icon of the Virgin Mary came up from the sea.

Much of the monastery was destroyed by fire in 1967, but the church itself remained undamaged until, in August 1974, the Turks bombarded it. Yet again the monastery had to be restored. I took a quick look at the icon. A lace curtain covered it and behind it I found the icon encased in silver, with a small silver door which could be opened to reveal an aperture through which a small portion of ancient wood could be seen. As I was in a devout frame of mind, I gave grateful thanks that I'd survived to see it.

An elderly monk sat outside the monastery shop and, when I spoke to him, I discovered he was the Abbot - Abbot Dionysios, founder of the monastery's icon conservation workshop. He told me he'd studied the subject of conservation in Constantinople (the Orthodox Church refers to Istanbul by its old Byzantine name), and also in Rome, before coming to Cyprus. When he saw I was interested, he unlocked an inner door and took me through to his workroom. Icons in every state of disrepair were ranged around the walls awaiting his attention. Many had been salvaged from the monastery fire, and others were split or partially cracked. He then opened a book on icons which displayed his name as the restorer of each. There was no pride, only humility in the fact that he had been chosen to undertake this painstaking task, and had the talent to do it.

I bought two bottles of monastery wine, noting that the Abbot's name was similar to Dionysos, god of wine. With my purchases I sat briefly on the monastery terrace. From it there was a stunning view over the pine forests and terraced vineyards to distant hills.

I was back with Harry before he'd had time to miss me. I found him still absorbed with the Cypriot struggle under the leadership of Archbishop Makarios. "Oh, hello," he said, "you've been quick!"

The Stoic decided to 'stick with it' beside the pool at our hotel. She was reading a historical romance and couldn't put it down. It was Friday evening and the start of a public holiday because of Pentecost (the coming of the Holy Spirit). The hotel was suddenly crowded with groups of thuggish looking yuppies, and British soldiers in swimming trunks, many with tattoos and hairy chests. They surrounded the pool accompanied by beauties in bikinis. Several transistors were turned on and, though muted, were persistent and couldn't be ignored.

Harry agreed to come with me to the next village to

see a museum - The Basket Museum. The Stoic raised her head and lowered her sun-glasses. "Is it advisable?" she enquired.

"Highly advisable," I replied, watching a couple applying suntan oil to each other. The hands were becoming more and more caressing under the influence of the goddess of love. I wondered if the waiters would intervene if the couple began to make love by the pool, but didn't wait to see.

The village of Inea was a small and typical Cypriot village. The road through it was narrow and, outside the café, the usual group of elders sat surveying the world. We were directed towards the church because, we were told, the museum was behind it. As we couldn't locate it, I asked at a small shop with the exaggerated title of 'supermarket'. The museum? Oh, it was closed, but that was no problem, they would telephone through and it would be opened for us.

When I translated this news to Harry, he immediately objected that we couldn't allow them to put themselves out on our behalf. But the man was already on the phone.

Soon I was far more interested in the fact that the nearby church was open, and many bent old women in black dresses, stockings and shoes, with black shawls over their heads, were coming slowly up the village street and entering the church. Each carried a plate on which was a round loaf of bread on a layer of grain, the kollyva (symbolic of burial and resurrection), with a lighted candle stuck into the loaf. A young woman from the Basket Museum came down to us. She had a welcoming, friendly face and spoke excellent English with an Australian accent. She had spent many years in Australia, she told us. I questioned her about the old women going to the church. "Yes, it is the start of the Kataklysma festival," she told me.

"Can I go in?" I asked, ignoring Harry's expression of dismay.

"Yes, of course."

"My husband is very interested in baskets and weaving," I said pleasantly. "I'll be back in a minute. I only want to see." And I was gone before Harry could object. There must have been about twenty old women in the church, except for one beauty of about thirty. Each laid her plate on the floor to the left of the iconostasis, then moved to the right where she joined others gathered around the priest. Some were already seated on chairs in the centre of the church and I joined them, aware that I was an object of curiosity. One by one the women came from the priest, bearing an incense cup from which a wreath of smoke rose. She then proffered her incense cup to those who were seated, and each passed a hand across the smoke. I did the same when it was offered to me. I would have liked to have stayed to see what happened next, but I felt I should rescue Harry.

I found him waiting patiently, having bought a thickly woven double-handled basket. The woman's youngest daughter had been filling it with her toys, and Harry had good-naturedly been selling them back to her.

I asked the mother more about the Kataklysma festival. She told me that this was an annual ritual, and the candles were to light the way for the souls of the dead. All were widows, and the younger beauty had lost her husband in a car accident a year earlier.

"So why did they pass incense around and want you to wave your hand across the smoke?" I enquired. I was told this wasn't incense but olive leaves being burned over charcoal.

"It is in order to wave away the evil spirits," said the woman.

"And the plate of kollyva and the round loaves," I asked, "are they symbolic of something?"

"The bread will be cut up into cubes and distributed, and the kollyva represents resurrection," came the reply.

"But why aren't there any men - any widowers?" I asked.

"They come another day. Tomorrow, or perhaps it is Sunday, they are invited to attend, and they all prostrate themselves for ten minutes."

I wished that I could witness this but, unfortunately, we were returning to Paphos. "So you won't be here on Monday?" enquired the young woman. "That is the day during the Kataklysma when you are in danger of having water thrown over you - eh, Maria?" And the woman fondled the head of her young daughter who hid her face in her skirts. "It is an old Christian custom here in Cyprus and is in memory of Noah and the Flood."

"Or of Aphrodite," I said. "At least that is what I've read. I've been told the custom is older than Christianity here on Cyprus."

"I do not know," said the woman.

When we left the village, Harry said, "So what was all that about, those women going to the church?"

"I gather they were praying for the souls of their dead and, presumably, since it's Pentecost, invoking the Holy Spirit's help."

Harry shrugged and said it was his guess they'd no idea what they were doing, but were just going through the motions which had been practised for centuries.

"That," I said with feeling, "could apply to all of us everywhere. We all latch onto the example set from the past and carry it forward with us, as though we daren't let it go. It's why we all celebrate Christmas, much of which is pagan with the increasing strength of the sun - or Easter which represents the revival of the Spirit of Corn. We all continue to play-act things we don't really believe. Why do we all do it?"

"I suppose the answer to that is why not?" came the reply. "Life would be very dull without festivals and celebrations."

To spare Harry the ordeal of more explorings in the ancient part of Paphos where St. Paul had preached, I went alone to the old port, and left him lying on the tourist beach. The Stoic was visiting a niece.

I managed to park the car along the sea-front which was a seething mass of stall-holders and people who'd come for the Kataklysma. But there at Paphos I saw nobody pouring water over anyone. All perambulated lazily along the sea-front drinking from cans, or licking ice-creams. I'd have welcomed a bucket of water because of the heat, and kept drinking bottled water and eating salted peanuts, aware of the possible consequences if I didn't.

I came to the old, typically Byzantine 13th century Church of Agia Kyriaki. It was to this area that St. Paul had come in c.45 A.D. Nearby was a pillar to which it is said, he'd been tied and given thirty-nine lashes, as punishment for preaching the Gospel.

For St. Paul, Cyprus must have been a horror story of lust and passion. In his Epistle to the Thessalonians - written from Corinth (another city of Aphrodite), St. Paul had warned the people to '...abstain from immorality;

that each one of you know how to take a wife for himself in holiness and honour, not in the passion of lust like heathen who do not know God...' Two thousand years on and Christians were taking each other in as much lust as ever. Humanity seemed little changed.

Paul, after his blinding light on the road to Damascus, found himself 'chosen' which made him one-eyed and focused forever, unlike those of us who are 'unchosen' and keep searching for the meaning of life.

I wondered if St. Paul knew about Aphrodite's annual festival, and the young girls at her temple; or the Rites of Adonis whose Adonia festival every year also commemorated death and resurrection. And, if he knew of them, did he pour scorn on them and condemn them? Or did the Cypriots, who already accepted the resurrection of Adonis, find it comparatively easy to take on board the Resurrection of Jesus, Son of the supreme God of the Jews, who fought battles for his 'chosen people', and could presumably do the same for his unchosen ones if they co-operated with this new Christian religion?

Hearing about the arrival of St. Paul in Paphos, the then Roman proconsul called him to his residence in order to discuss religion. He had with him a brilliant Jewish theosophist called Bar-Jesus ('theosophist' means philosopher professing a knowledge of God). According to the Gospels, Bar-Jesus had been no match for St. Paul who (to quote from the Acts of the Apostles) was 'filled with the Holy Spirit, looked intently at him and said, "You son of the devil, you enemy of all righteousness, full of all deceit and villainy, will you not stop making crooked the straight paths of the Lord?" ' And, without any more ado, he called down on him divine anger which struck him blind. In a panic the proconsul was immediately converted to Christianity.

"You'd have been the first convert under the circumstances," Harry remarked later when I told him the story.

"Yes, I would, but not from conviction, only from fear," I admitted. "I don't call that a good enough reason for faith - blind faith!"

"Is that where the saying comes from?" Harry asked, preparing to go into the sea for another swim.

"Could be," I replied.

"I'll come if you think it will help," said the Stoic's niece, when her aunt told her that if she couldn't get pregnant by her lawful wedded husband, then she should come with us to the Troodhitissa Monastery where they had a fertility girdle.

"We're going there anyway," said the Stoic, "so this is your big opportunity." And she gathered her niece into an embrace, declaring that everything must be done to help her become a great-aunt.

We drove up into the Troodos Mountains and weaved our way along a well surfaced tarmac road flanked by pine forests, till we reached this isolated monastery perched on the mountain side. Beside the car park was a notice which said 'No Tourists Admitted'. This was an unexpected blow. We watched a group of Germans walk down some steps to the entrance, only to be turned back by the monk on duty.

"So what now?" asked the Stoic.

"Rules are rules," said Harry.

"They're general guidelines, not laws," I remarked.

Harry walked resolutely back to the car. With a

hunching of shoulders and despairing wave of both arms, he indicated that he would have nothing more to do with us if we chose to defy the order.

The Stoic and her niece came down the steps with me, and I approached the monk and said in the best Greek I was able to gather, that we had come all the way up to their monastery because we understood they had a girdle, and that my friend here - and I brought forward the niece who smiled and blushed.

"Ah, you have a problem?" said the young monk with a look of compassion.

"Yes, she has a problem."

"Ah. Wait a minute please." And the young monk consulted with a colleague.

We were invited into the main church. The place exuded holiness. There was a beautifully carved pulpit painted in Renaissance blues and greens, as was the iconostasis with its many icons in ancient gilded frames. The lighting came from chandeliers with huge crystal drops reflecting all the colours of the rainbow. The wonder-working icon of the Virgin Mary was to the left of the Royal Doors.

This icon is said to have also floated across the sea, to get away from the eighth century Iconoclast controversy. On its arrival at Cyprus, it had been rescued by two hermits who brought it to their cave. In due course they had died, and the icon lay forgotten. In the thirteenth century, the icon began to glow in a strange manner, alerting people to its whereabouts, and the monastery was eventually founded in its honour. The icon and the girdle were invoked for fertility, something which had originally been the province of Aphrodite.

I pointed out the icon to the Stoic and her niece, and showed them how to make the sign of the cross the

Orthodox way. It wasn't long before a monk of about thirty entered and disappeared into the sanctuary. He re-emerged with an ancient, dark velvet and gold encrusted belt, which he gave to the Stoic's niece to put around her waist. We then left her alone before the icon, and the monk joined us by the church entrance. He began to tell us in excellent English how he'd studied theology for three years at the London Polytechnic. It rather surprised me, as I didn't think theology could be studied there.

The relics of a saint, he said, were his soul and body and very powerful; to honour them was the first step towards God. He spoke very naturally and with assurance. I asked how it was that he'd become a monk, and he replied that he had felt himself chosen by God, and had such love in his heart for him, that he could do no more with his life than to serve him. It was a fascinating admission.

After about ten minutes, the Stoic's niece returned looking serene, and the girdle was returned to the young monk. Money? No, no, it was a gift. We felt very humble and reverential. The chameleon in me was totally at one with this holy setting.

We bowed our way out, speaking in hushed monosyllables and wearing holiness like an all enveloping cloak. We found Harry seated in the car with the door open. Seeing us approach he got out, dubious as to what to say to women newly emerged from a holy experience. He threw me a tentative, assessing sort of look then, satisfied that I appeared more or less normal, got back into the driving seat and gave a polite cough.

The Stoic was more forthright. "Interesting! We await events!"

Her niece eventually said: "When I put on that girdle, there was an extraordinary feeling of warmth which passed through me."

"Most certainly we await events!" said the prospective great-aunt with enthusiasm.

That evening Harry and I had supper alone at a taverna near the quayside. The Stoic was spending the evening with her niece and friends. Because of the Kataklysma festival, there was music and dancing at the end of the quay below the floodlit medieval castle. The setting was romantic with each table lit by a candle in a glass chimney. A full moon hung in the night sky, casting its silvery shimmering light along the sea where the goddess of love had risen from the waves.

"A moon?" said Harry who had his back to it. "Oh, so there is." And he returned to his food and brought the candle closer, to make sure he was eating what he'd ordered and not a dead beetle or any other suspect object. Having satisfied himself that all was well, he settled down to his grilled fish, every now and then lifting his candle up to inspect it.

"I don't know why people like candle-light," he remarked, "I like to see what I'm eating," and he poked about at his plate.

"I think it's really romantic."

"Hell, a fish-bone!" And Harry was silent as he manoeuvred the bone into a position where he could extract it.

Whilst Harry was salvaging the bone, a young gypsy girl came to the taverna with an armful of red roses, each individually wrapped. She came up to our table and put a rose in front of Harry. Ever the romantic, I hoped I would be presented with it. Harry, however, thought the girl had given him his table-napkin from the ground, and said 'thank you'. Had he had a better light he might have seen it was a rose. Hastily, I pointed out his mistake and, as the child hovered with her outstretched palm, and I waited hopefully, Harry, seeing it wasn't something to wipe his mouth on, returned the rose to the child. I must have shown disappointment because Harry said: "You didn't want it, did you?"

"Not really. Aphrodite's island and all that, it would have been quite nice."

"What on earth would you do with a rose?" he asked.

"Well - "

"If you really want one - but I don't think you do - "

"No, I don't think I do, not really - But - "

"I'll buy you one, if you have to have one. But where would you put it?"

"Tooth mug?"

"Do we have a tooth mug?"

By now the gypsy girl was far away, plying her trade amongst those of a more romantic disposition. As lovers looked into each others eyes, and roses were purchased and offered to young girls (and old ones), by moonlight and candle-light, I looked thoughtfully at Harry who had found another bone. The gypsy girl, who'd forgotten she'd already approached us, came again, and this time Harry rose to the occasion. But he wouldn't speak to her, and told me with a flourish of largesse to 'get that rose if I really wanted it.'

"No, you get it if you'd like to give it to me."

What an impasse. The girl saw she was onto a lost cause and was soon once more gone into the night.

The following day we returned to Larnaka. We were a few miles from the city, and I was at the wheel and, therefore, in a position of power, when the Stoic said: "We're approaching the Halla Sultan Tekke Mosque on our left."

"Mercifully my wife's not interested in mosques," said Harry confidently.

I saw the signpost flash by and, realizing it was my only opportunity, I did a smart about turn, ignoring the sharp intake of breath from Harry, and aware that the Stoic, though remaining outwardly calm, gripped the seat and put her foot on an imaginary brake.

I knew that in the Moslem world this mosque was one of the most important shrines after Mecca, Medina and Jerusalem. I informed the others of this fact, and told them how it marked the spot where Muhammed's maternal aunt had fallen from a mule and broken her neck.

"A broken neck from a mule is one thing, dear, but to risk all our necks in a car is something else," rebuked the Stoic mildly.

"I'd rather ride a mule than be in a car driven by one," said Harry with feeling.

I ignored these remarks as we drew up in the car park. We walked along a stretch of dusty track, through a so-called garden to the small mosque, which nestled amongst palms and cypresses beside the Salt Lake, a source of commercial salt since antiquity. I covered my head, took off my sandals and walked over an ancient marble step into the domed edifice. It was the first time I had been in a mosque.

For some while I had been toying with the thought of Islam, and was even playing with the idea of learning Arabic. If anybody were to ask me 'why?' I had no answer, except that the urge was on me. So far I hadn't mentioned it to Harry. It was, I supposed, all part of my search for a divine and ultimate being.

It had been at a service the previous Christmas, whilst I was doing the Christian thing of going through the motions of belief, that I had suddenly considered looking into Judaism and Islam. It struck me during the sermon that it was extraordinary that I was sitting there, listening attentively to a man in the pulpit, who was being paid to speak about things which seemed quite unbelievable. It then occurred to me that if I found Christianity difficult then, perhaps, my only problem was that I'd been born into the wrong tradition. The God in Judaism and Islam presented a whole new vista to be explored.

I looked around the small mosque which, compared to an Orthodox Church, was totally bare, and noted the mihrab, which was the niche to be found in all mosques pointing the direction of Mecca. Nearby was a heavy slab, marking the spot where Muhammed's maternal aunt had been buried. That she was directly related to the Prophet was the reason for the shrine's importance.

Yes, I would study Arabic and learn about the Islamic faith. I would visit Egypt, Turkey and other Middle Eastern countries. I knew Harry wouldn't want to come, but neither would he like it if he stayed behind.

We left the mosque and drove back to Larnaka, this time with Harry at the wheel as he didn't want to be driven by a certain 'you-know-what'. The Salt Lake on our left lay still like frozen ice; at its centre was a sheet of mirror-like water reflecting wisps of high evening cloud. The mosque could be glimpsed over the far side amongst its palm trees and cypresses.

We had a party that evening to celebrate the end of our journey and as a farewell to the Stoic. After several glasses of wine I began to speak recklessly and give voice to my new plans.

"If your wife wants to ride camels through the desert and study Islam then you must let her," the Stoic said to Harry.

Harry replied, "She doesn't want to really. She gets these odd notions."

When we said good-bye the Stoic murmured in my ear, "If you do have some way-out plan, I'll come with you if Harry won't."

"I'll remember that," I said.

As the engines revved and the plane speeded along the runway for take-off, Harry said: "Well, here goes! Say your prayers!"

I became aware that we were in the air and rising. Aphrodite's island receded from us, but her myths and loves remained embedded in my head. It was odd to think that these stories had been spun out down the centuries for over three thousand years.

"Soon be back!" said Harry, settling himself comfortably as he adjusted his seat to the reclining position and closed his eyes.

"We hope!" I remarked. I expected to get home but, in a strange contrariwise way, knew there was always the risk that we mightn't.

"Oh, speaking of hope, I quite forgot!" said Harry,

suddenly sitting up. He leaned forward and rummaged in his zip bag, and withdrew a wilted rather crumpled red rose which he presented to me.

"Good heavens!" I said, "a battered red rose, how lovely!"

"She said I could pick it from her garden," said Harry with satisfaction, having done the romantic thing, if rather late.

I put my nose to the wilting bloom which didn't smell of rose but of socks, and the petals promptly scattered leaving me with a stalk. Harry's gesture, though, spoke volumes, as we flew off into the dawn from the island of the goddess of love, and headed for whatever more the future held for us.

THE END

GLOSSARY OF GODS & HEROES

ADONIS

A handsome youth who was adored by Aphrodite, goddess of love. He was killed whilst hunting wild boar.

AEGISTHUS

Seducer of Clytemnestra, wife of King Agamemnon. He helped Clytemnestra to murder her husband when he returned from the Trojan War.

AGAMEMNON

King of Mycenae and leader of the Achaeans (Greeks) in the Trojan War.

ALEXANDER THE GREAT

(356-323 B.C.) King of Macedonia, son of Philip II and Olympias. He was a keen admirer of Homer's Iliad and carried a copy of it with him throughout his campaigns.

APHRODITE

Goddess of love.

APOLLO

Son of Zeus and Leto, and twin brother of Artemis. He was god of music, archery and prophecy.

ARIADNE

Daughter of King Minos of Crete. She devised a plan by which Theseus was able to kill the Minotaur after which she sailed away with him to the island of Naxos in the Aegean where she was later abandoned.

ARTEMIS

Daughter of Zeus and Leto, and twin sister of Apollo. She was goddess of wild life and hunting and was also identified with the moon.

ASCLEPIUS
God of medicine, son of Apollo and a mortal woman.

ATHENA
Daughter of Zeus. She was virgin goddess of wisdom, arts and crafts, and patron goddess of Athens.

CLYTEMNESTRA
Wife of Agamemnon, king of Mycenae, and sister of Helen.

DEMETER
Goddess of corn and agriculture.

DIOMEDES
Leader of the men of Argos against the Trojans.

DIONYSOS
Son of Zeus and the mortal woman, Semele. He was god of wine and drama.

EILEITHYIA
A minor goddess who presided over childbirth.

EURYDICE
A beautiful nymph who married Orpheus and died tragically soon afterwards from a snake bite.

FURIES
The Greek spirits of vengeance who harassed those who had committed murder within their family. They were often portrayed as winged women, and could be regarded as symbolizing pangs of conscience.

GAEA
Personification of the earth.

HADES
Brother of Zeus and god of the underworld.

HELEN

The beautiful wife of Menelaus, king of Sparta. She was seduced by Paris and ran away with him to Troy which triggered the Trojan War (See Judgement of Paris).

HELIOS

A Greek sun-god who was later identified with Apollo.

HERA

Wife of Zeus, goddess of women and marriage.

HERCULES

Best known of the Greek heroes for his twelve labours, and renowned for his courage, strength, endurance and compassion.

HIPPOLYTUS

Son of Theseus and the Amazon queen, Hippolyta, with whom Theseus' second wife, Phaedra, fell hopelessly in love with disastrous consequences.

HORAE

Three minor goddesses representing the seasons. They were sometimes identified with the Graces.

HYDRA

A many-headed monster which Hercules was given to kill as his second labour. His chief problem was that when one head was lopped off, another grew in its place.

IRIS

Goddess of the rainbow and messenger of the gods.

JUDGEMENT OF PARIS

A legend in which Strife, during the course of a marriage-feast, threw down a golden apple inscribed with the words 'for the fairest'. The three goddesses, Aphrodite, Athena and Hera, each thought the apple was intended for her and it was left to Paris, son of the King of Troy, to decide who was to receive it. Each of the goddesses offered him a bribe to persuade him to choose her and he settled for Aphrodite as she promised him Helen, the most beautiful woman in the world.

LETO

A minor goddess, daughter of the Titans who were the offspring of Uranus (heaven) and Gaea (earth). She was mother of Apollo and Artemis by Zeus.

MINOTAUR

A monstrous creature half man, half bull, the child of Pasiphae, daughter of Helios the sun-god, and wife of King Minos of Crete. The god Poseidon caused her to become enamoured of a bull in order to punish King Minos for refusing to sacrifice the bull to him.

MUSES

Nine daughters of Zeus and Mnemosyne (personification of Memory). Each presided over one of the arts or sciences.

NAIADS

Nymphs of springs, rivers and lakes, usually gentle and beautiful, but some could be malevolent.

ORESTES

Son of King Agamemnon and Clytemnestra. He was hounded by the Furies after he killed his mother in order to avenge her murder of his father.

ORPHEUS

Founder of the mystic cult of Orphism. He was the son of one of the Muses and possibly Apollo, and became renowned for charming wild beasts with his singing. He married Eurydice and was distraught when she died soon afterwards from a snake bite.

PAN

A minor god of shepherds and flocks, part man, part goat, who roamed about the mountains playing his seven reeds pipe which he had invented.

PANDORA

The first woman to be created. She came with a box containing all the evils of the world. When it was opened they all escaped, leaving only Hope at the bottom to alleviate men's sorrows.

PARIS

Son of the King of Troy. Aphrodite helped him to seduce the beautiful Helen which caused the Trojan War (see Judgement of Paris).

PERSEPHONE

Daughter of Demeter. She was a beautiful young goddess who was abducted and carried off to the underworld by Hades and became his queen.

PHAEDRA

Daughter of King Minos of Crete, and sister of Ariadne. She became the wife of Theseus and fell in love with Hippolytus, her step-son, with tragic consequences.

POSEIDON

Brother of Zeus. He was god of the sea as well as of earthquakes and horses.

SEMELE

A mortal woman with whom Zeus fell in love. She was the mother of Dionysos.

STOICS

A school of philosophy founded by Zeno c.315 B.C. Zeno thought that the aim of man was happiness which could only be achieved by right conduct in harmony with nature. This, he claimed, was the law of the universe.

THESEUS

Legendary King of Athens who, before coming to the throne, killed the Minotaur in its Labyrinth with the help of Ariadne, King Minos of Crete's daughter.

TROJAN WAR

A war waged by the Achaeans (Greeks) against the Trojans in order to recover Helen who had run off with Paris, son of the King of Troy.

ZENO

Founder of the Stoic school of philosophy in Athens c.315 B.C. He came from Cyprus.

ZEUS

Supreme god of the ancient world. God of the heavens and controller of the weather. In classical times he was regarded as protector of civic law and justice.

ALSO BY
JILL DUDLEY
HOLY SMOKE!
TRAVELS IN TURKEY
AND EGYPT

JILL DUDLEY'S
YE GODS! II
MORE TRAVELS IN GREECE
EXPLORES THE PAGAN
SANCTUARIES